...but we need the eggs

THE MAGIC OF WOODY ALLEN

...but we need the eggs

THE MAGIC OF WOODY ALLEN

By DIANE JACOBS

St. Martin's Press   New York

For Gerry

Library of Congress Cataloging in Publication Data
Jacobs, Diane.
    But we need the eggs.
    1. Allen, Woody. I.Title.
PN2287.A53j3   791.43′028′0924   81-23201
ISBN 0-312-10998-9   AACR2

Design by Kingsley Parker

10 9 8 7 6 5 4 3 2 1

Contents

A section of photographs follows page 114.

Acknowledgments

I would like to thank the following people and organizations for their help in providing prints of the films, illustrations, and support: Lance Bird, Peter Cowie, Armando DelTorto, Films for the Humanities, Films Inc., Nathan Goldman, Albert J. LaValley, Harold Mantell, the Library of Congress, Photoreporters, Beryl Schatz, Swank Films, United Artists, and John Wang. My especial thanks to my editors Les Pockell and Susan Tennenbaum for their perceptions and suggestions; to Woody Allen and Norma Lee Clark for their cooperation; to Dennis Higgins, then at United Artists, for assistance way beyond the call of duty; to my most industrious agent and friend, Howard Morhaim; and, most of all, to Gerry Rabkin, without whose patience, support, insights and standard of excellence I could never have written this book.

After that it got pretty late, and we both had to go. But it was great seeing Annie again. I realized what a terrific person she was and how much fun it was just knowing her. And I thought of that old joke, you know, that this guy goes to a psychiatrist, and he says, "Doc, my brother's crazy, he thinks he's a chicken." And, ah, the doctor says, "Well, why don't you turn him in?" And the guy says, "I would but I need the eggs." Well, I guess that's pretty much now how I feel about relationships. You know, they're totally irrational and crazy and absurd and . . . but, I guess we keep going through it because, ah, most of us need the eggs. . . .

Annie Hall

=1=

Enter Woody

A small, red-haired, bespectacled man in his mid-twenties squints from the center of the stage. He seems to have recently shed weight. His too-large sports jacket looks ready to swallow him up, and his darting, sorrowful eyes obviously hope it will —quickly. Mentally, he's chewed his fingernails to the bone, and still the feet can't stop shuffling.

Then, the voice. The thin, raspy New York voice that doesn't quite mesh with the image:

> This is my—ah—third night here. I haven't been here in about eight months. And—ah—since I was here last a lot of significant things have occurred in my private life that I thought we could go over tonight. And—um—evaluate. I moved—let me start at the beginning. Ah, I lived in Manhattan, uptown east, in a brownstone building. But I was constantly getting mugged and assaulted. Um—sadistically beaten about the face and neck. So I moved into a doorman apartment house on Park Avenue that's rich and secure and expensive and great, and I lived there two weeks, and my doorman attacked me . . .

In the early sixties the anomaly of Woody Allen was still a surprise. Who was this small, alienated Jewish man, so vulnerable he was "constantly getting mugged and assaulted," yet so resilient (and wealthy) he lived to get attacked by his own Park Avenue doorman? What could be made of a fellow who, in various other nightclub routines, was so susceptible he got hypnotized by "The Ed Sullivan Show"; so eloquent he sold the Ku Klux Klan Israel bonds; so gullible he accepted an ant as a watch dog; yet so audacious he debated literature with Ernest Hemingway? Above all, who was this weaver of outrageous— but logical—fantasies, this very clever writer?

Woody Allen has come a long way since the early nightclub days. He's distinguished himself in five careers—as nightclub performer, prose writer, actor, playwright, and film writer/director. He's written three full-length plays; published three collections of short writings; acted in *What's New, Pussycat?*, *Casino Royale,* and *The Front,* as well as in his own dramatic vehicles; and directed nine feature films. And since, as Sandy Bates in *Stardust Memories* explains to a less fortunate ex-classmate, "our society places a great value on jokes," he's been well honored. His 1977 short story "The Kugelmass Episode" won an O. Henry Award; *Annie Hall* won four Oscars; and his plays as well as his movies have found a wide and faithful audience throughout the world. Now Woody Allen is to us what Napoleon is to Boris in *Love and Death:* "a famous human being, a successful one, one who earns more than I do."

And yet he remains Woody Allen, the man who for two decades has sustained a love affair with contemporary audiences: making us laugh, cry, think; insisting that we identify with him—that, in the words of film critic Richard Schickel, "Woody, c'est moi," for us all.

Who precisely is Woody Allen? The question is deceptively simple, for there are at least three sometimes indistinguishable Woody Allens. There is, most accessibly, the Woody Allen "persona"—the character who stares at us from nightclub rostrum, stage, or screen and whom, for convenience's sake, we'll call Woody. Woody is Woody Allen's symbolic self—the slight, Jewish, schnooky but smart New Yorker who began dramatic life at the hungry i and the Village Vanguard in the early sixties and grew up to be, among other things, a miserable divorcé (in *Play It Again, Sam*), a failed crook (in *Take the Money and Run*), a sperm (in *Everything You Always Wanted to Know about Sex*) and, more recently, a world renowned filmmaker (in *Stardust Memories*). Whatever his guise of the moment, Woody is true to his essential anomalousness. Buffeted by the traumas, plagued by the anxieties of modern urban existence—the Park Avenue doormen! the Godlessness!—he can no more triumph than he can stop trying. As a lover, he beguiles us with his foibles—do you feel small? He *is* smaller. Are you maladroit? He's downright klutzy—intensifying, and thus at once dignifying and palliating, our own shortcomings. As a metaphor, he has come to embody the struggles of late twentieth-century urban man.

But the Woody persona is only one face of Woody Allen. There is also Woody Allen the creator, whom we'll call Allen, who breathes life into Woody and then proceeds to manipulate him: to turn his bungling inadequacies into gleeful ironies, or to transform his special predicament into an artist's distinctive vision of the world. Even in the early club routines, author makes a point of distancing himself from performer. "These things really happen to me," confesses Woody after an especially improbable anecdote, and we know he speaks exclusively for his fictional self. These things don't *really* happen to Allen the artist. Or do they? And, more important, do author and character *feel* the same way about "these things"? Do they speak with a single voice? Throughout the years, as Allen's art has grown darker, the gap between artist and character has widened; yet, the dramatic impact of this discrepancy remains constant. In *Stardust Memories* as in *Play It Again, Sam,* Allen *uses* his protagonist's ambiguous identity to complicate and deepen narrative conflicts.

And similarly, both Allen and Woody use the third face of Woody Allen, Mr. Allen, the famous man. You may have missed the latest Woody Allen film, but have you seen the morning papers, the talk shows? Then surely you know that Mr. Allen plays clarinet every Monday night at Michael's Pub, that he drives—no, is driven in—a Rolls-Royce, that he wears his celebrity like an albatross and thinks little of the comic gift which has brought him fame and fortune. If you buy the Sunday *Times,* you are doubtless aware that while Woody is far too spontaneous (if not poor) to bother about his furniture, Mr. Allen has spent hours and days with an interior decorator, carefully selecting tasteful furniture for his condominium overlooking Central Park.

Does this have anything to do with the art of Woody Allen? Most certainly. For, ever since the early seventies, and the tremendous popularity of the club acts and *Play It Again, Sam,* Mr. Allen the celebrity has been part of our national consciousness, subtly affecting our attitude toward every aspect of his work. We were not altogether surprised when Woody, that terrible loser, won the girl—Louise Lasser—in *Bananas* because we knew Mr. Allen had been married to her in real life. We were doubly sorry when Woody and Diane Keaton parted in *Annie Hall* because hadn't they parted in real life as well?

So Mr. Allen adds a third and important dimension to the anomaly of Woody Allen. He is also "his" articulate spokesman. Shortly after the opening of *The Floating Lightbulb* he agreed to meet with me, and our long and illuminating interview will be referred to time and again throughout this book.

But, for the most part, the work will speak for itself. For this is a study of the creative voyage of Woody Allen: from his beginnings in the popular art of stand-up comedy, through the early essays, plays, and films, and into the mature work. Allen's growth has certainly been remarkable—who could have imagined that the man who directed *Take the Money and Run* would one day be compared to Ingmar Bergman and Preston Sturges?—but no more remarkable than his fundamental consistency. From first to last (with notable exceptions, such as *Interiors*), his principal subject matter has been himself—as artist, as character, as celebrity. And while peripheral themes have come and gone, the obsessions that were with him in the nightclub acts are still with him today. These obsessions have mostly to do with the incongruity of things. Why can't the body perform what the mind can conceive—such as immortality? Why can't experience imitate the perfection of art? Why is the ideal always so much finer than the practice?

Mind? Body? Ideal? Practice? Woody Allen's groan is almost

audible, as these are, indeed, just the sort of abstractions he's spent a lifetime punching holes in. But no apologies to him, for they are also—and again incongruously—the abstractions he has most powerfully employed. The world's cleverest debunker of the intellectual is himself a closet intellectual; the artist who mercilessly parodies the abstruse is also the artist who unabashedly reveres it. Madness? Or perhaps what F. Scott Fitzgerald described as genius: the ability to hold two ideas in the mind at the same time and still retain the ability to function.

As subverter of his own deepest concerns, Woody Allen is not an easy man to write about, but he's a fascinating challenge, and most fascinating in his contradictions. And nowhere are these contradictions more profound than in the dramatic conflict which, throughout his varied career, has pulled his most important ideas into a meaningful vision. And this conflict, in most general terms, is between reality—or life as it is—and magic—or life as one's (usually Woody's) mind and imagination can transform it.

For Allen, reality is all the gloomy things that can descend upon his vulnerable protagonist: getting attacked by the Park Avenue doorman as described in the nightclub act; being drafted to fight Napoleon in *Love and Death;* losing Annie in *Annie Hall.* As in the Groucho Marx joke (evoked at the start of *Annie Hall*) about the food in a Catskill hotel, reality is awful, and such small portions! Magic, on the other hand, is life's loophole, its escape valve, the sleight of hand (one's own or someone else's) which turns reality into something funnier, lovelier, less painful, or at the very least different. Magic is the literal legerdemain of Father Drobney in Allen's first play and of the child magician Paul in his latest. But it is also Woody's daydream in the club monologues, Renata's art in *Interiors,* and the romantic love which descends from the heavens and releases almost every Woody Allen protagonist from the miseries of modern existence for a little while.

Though more joyful in Allen's early work, this conflict between magic and reality is never a simple one, and thus its nuances are best appreciated in relation to the specific works themselves. But before turning to these works in chronological sequence, let us peek quickly toward the end of the road at

Allen's 1977 *New Yorker* story, "The Kugelmass Episode." In contrast to his early, flamboyantly satirical essays, the tone of this brief allegory is quiet, almost rueful. The gist of the plot is that Kugelmass, an unhappily remarried humanities professor at City College and chronic analysand, is fed up with life and his women. His new wife has grown fat and grouchy and, what's more, isn't so new. Kugelmass wants to make love in Venice, to dine by candlelight. "I'm a man who needs romance," he whines to long-time analyst Dr. Mandel, who replies that he's not a magician.

So Kugelmass leaves prosaic Dr. Mandel ("An affair will solve nothing," says he, " . . . your problems run much deeper.") in search of magic, and finds the Great Persky, conjurer of art and romance. Enter Persky's cabinet with the novel of your choice, and you can live in it—and with its heroine—for as long as you please. Then give a yell, and Persky brings you back to reality. Francophilic Kugelmass chooses *Madame Bovary* and begins dropping in on Emma in the nineteenth-century French countryside the way he used to visit Dr. Mandel. Only Emma is much more fun; in fact, she's so much fun he arranges for Persky to summon her to twentieth-century New York for a whirlwind weekend at the Plaza Hotel, after which the fun stops because Persky can't get her back into the book.

Now Kugelmass has not only a routine job, a greedy ex-wife, and a nagging, increasingly suspicious current spouse to contend with, but he has Emma Bovary demanding marriage or a return ticket to Flaubert. By the time Persky gets Emma back home, Kugelmass has learned his lesson. No more magic for him—from now on, it's reality all the time. "I'll never cheat again, I swear it," he assures Persky. Three weeks later, he's back in the cabinet.

"The Kugelmass Episode" is a kind of "rosebud" for Woody Allen. That reality daunts and bores, love fades, God is dead, and politics are futile have been his messages from the start. But for all its deficiencies, magic sustains—as we shall see.

=2=

Getting Started

The Nightclub Acts

It is fitting that the creator of Kugelmass and other reality-bound escapists should have found his first vocation in magic.

Woody Allen was born Alan Stewart Konigsberg in Brooklyn, New York, on December 1, 1935. By his own account, an indifferent student who excelled at legerdemain, Allen, like sixteen-year-old Paul in *The Floating Lightbulb,* escaped the routine of Brooklyn high school activity to visit magic stores in Manhattan. Also like Paul, he was a diligent escapist. According to biographer Eric Lax, for every hour he didn't study his math, he'd spend six learning and practicing card tricks. Magic, Allen told Lax, "kept me from the world"; as did vaudeville shows, any and all comedy acts, and movies (the Marx Brothers, Bob Hope, Ernst Lubitsch and Preston Sturges were favorites); though, in contrast to such film-aficionado peers as George Lucas, Steven Spielberg, and Martin Scorcese, he did not lose himself in the womb of the movie theater at every available moment. And, conspicuously unlike Woody the klutz, Allen was an enthusiastic athlete who would later, in the documentary *Woody Allen: An American Comedy,* insist that if he could live his life again he would pursue a physical career, such as baseball, which he played well.

Beyond his extracurricular talents, Allen displayed early in life a flair for comic writing, and by fifth grade was composing parodic stories in the pompous voice of his *Getting Even* narrators: "I would be doing references to Freud and sex . . . without knowing who he or what it really was," he told Lax. In high school he began sending off gags to the newspapers and at seventeen saw his first words in print in the Earl Wilson and Walter Winchell columns. A year later, under a twenty-five-dollar-a-week contract for the David O. Alber public relations firm, Allen was creating up to fifty jokes a day for such illustrious clients as Bob Hope, Arthur Murray, Guy Lombardo, and Sammy Kaye.

After graduating without distinction from Midwood High School, Woody Allen spent a single semester at New York University, majoring in film not, he assures me, with any career goal in mind, but because it was an easy course—"though I failed it." Nonetheless, Allen would soon turn the pain and boredom of formal education to imaginative use. In an early nightclub monologue he describes flunking out of college because he was caught cheating on his metaphysics test: "I looked within the soul of the boy sitting next to me."

Of course, academic failures cost Mr. Allen neither love nor money. But he *was* expelled from college after one semester, and he didn't, in the pleading words of *The Floating Lightbulb*'s Jewish mother (doubtless echoing Allen's own), "apply" himself. After leaving New York University, Allen just as briefly attended City College night courses, and in the late fifties, while he was writing for Sid Caesar, hired a tutor to coach him at home. Finally, he educated himself, with much-publicized concentrations in love and death, but this was long after he'd been hailed as America's leading intellectual comedian. ("I hated that appellation," Allen tells me, "and it's not true. Sahl is an intellectual, Mike Nichols is an intellectual—not me. You know, there's the old joke about the Jewish woman who says, 'My son is a general.' And the second woman says, 'To you he's a general and to me he's a general—but to a general he's a general?' ").

While still in his late teens, Allen the delinquent student was sent to Hollywood as the youngest member of NBC's Writer's Program, and there his personal and professional lives as an adult began. He married New Yorker Harlene Rosen, whom he had known since high school, and under professional guidance learned the lucrative business of television comedy writing, whose more banal aspects *Annie Hall* and *Manhattan* would scathingly parody. The strongest positive influence on Allen's career at this time was Danny Simon, Neil Simon's brother, of whom Allen told Lax, "I've learned a couple of things on my own since and modified things [Simon] told me, but everything, unequivocally, that I learned about comedy writing, I learned from him."

By the time Allen returned to New York in the late fifties, he was a well-known and respected comedy writer whose work appeared regularly on "The Ed Sullivan Show," Sid Caesar's Show and "The Tonight Show." But he was now beginning to chafe at the prospect of writing for another comic's glory, and like Kugelmass, he was restless with his life and wife.

In 1960, Allen and Harlene separated. According to an early routine, they chose divorce over a Bermuda holiday because, "the vacation is over in two weeks, but a divorce is something you have forever." And in the same year, with encouragement from his managers Jack Rollins and Charles H. Joffe, Allen began performing his own material at small Manhattan clubs like The Village Vanguard and The Blue Angel.

The vibrant stand-up-comedy community Allen entered in the early sixties was a generation removed from the Borscht Belt circuit. Change was in the air, and the improvisation experiments of Chicago's Second City and Compass theaters were spilling into nightclub performances as well. The fifties had seen the emergence of Nichols and May, Mort Sahl, and Lenny Bruce: all Jewish, and yet with a vision of ethnicity which differed pointedly from that of Henny Youngman or Milton Berle. Around these newer performers had gathered a young, Bohemian, college-educated, and often political audience which appreciated not only the joke per se, but its intellectual and social context and the raw, *seeming* spontaneity of the material. In small clubs all over urban America, Henny Youngman's "Take my wife—please!" was giving way to Nichols and May's "We would like to do something in the style of Pirandello."

Mike Nichols's description of the ideal Compass theater

performer (in *Something Wonderful Now*) applies to all these
new comedians: ". . . he has what few actors have—a sense of
character observed from without. The ability to comment on a
character with some humor and a little bit of distance and, at
its highest, with genius, like Elaine [May]: to be able simultaneously to comment from without and fill from within . . ." As
Nichols suggests, personality was as crucial to this performer
as to Youngman or Bob Hope, and yet, unlike the traditional
comedian, he sought references beyond himself, home, and
work, and often beyond the concerns of the average American.
Intellectual allusions abounded, though often they were no
more substantive than fifth-grader Allen's allusions to sex and
Freud.

As Paul Mazursky recalls the Second City improvisations of
this era, "Some [of the humor] was like what Bob Hope would
do when he toured for the troops—he'd toss in references to
generals and commanders . . . and the soldiers would scream
with the shock of recognition. At Second City, the same thing
applied, only the name you would drop would be Kierkegaard."
Still, whatever its substance, the appurtenances of this comedy
were such that a smart, urban Jewish analysand could really
connect with it.

Allen was especially inspired by Mort Sahl's "jazz-like" style
and intellectual arrogance. "My interest in nightclub performing was nil until I saw him," Allen told Lax. "Then it occurred
to me that 'Hey, you could be a comedian because you have the
equipment; that is a very valid way to express yourself.' " But
he was equally influenced by the comic timing and schnook
persona of the more traditional Bob Hope, of whom he has said,
"There are certain moments when I think he's the best thing
I've ever seen. It's everything I can do at certain times not to
actually do him." So together Sahl and Hope impelled Allen
toward his nightclub debut.

As Jack Rollins recalls the event: "He was so tense and
nervous that he kept fiddling with the [microphone] until we
thought he would choke himself." And Allen's first two years
as stand-up comic were continually tense; not, Allen explains,
because audiences were unreceptive. "I was a success from the
first time I hit the stage," he recalls. "I never worked on timing

and delivery because those are natural. But I was scared, and I worked at feeling more at ease and getting to enjoy my time on stage." And as he had practiced his magic tricks, Allen worked at perfecting his act, conferring with the supportive Rollins and Joffe after every performance. In *When the Shooting Stops,* Allen's film editor Ralph Rosenblum alludes to a trait which must have helped him through this difficult period: "Woody seemed to understand that as long as he had the ultimate authority he didn't have to fear the opinion of others. He was always ready to try it your way, and if your way succeeded, so much the better."

By 1963 Woody Allen had established a national reputation. The *Saturday Evening Post* headlined an enthusiastic profile of Allen, "Bright New Comic Clowns Toward Success." *Time* magazine described him as "a flat-headed, red-headed lemur with closely bitten fingernails and a sports jacket"; and, in the winter of 1963, "not only an interesting new comedian but a rare one as well; he never mentions John F. Kennedy." In a *Horizon* magazine profile, Charles L. Mee calls Woody "the pathetic little creature who gets up from the barroom floor again and again and again; he will never stay down, he will never conquer, and he will never give up." In short, "there's no way out for the character Woody Allen presents us."

If none of these early descriptions adequately evokes the complexity of the character Richard Schickel would later call "a walking compendium of a generation's concerns, comically stated," they all attest to the establishment of a distinct personality behind the gags, buzz words, and fantasies. With his tendency to daydream as a distinguishing trait, the early Woody persona had more in common with the traditional stand-up comic persona than with Nichols and May, Sahl, or Bruce. Though a mother-in-law was conspicuously absent, he told the stingy parent joke (learning that Woody's been kidnapped, his parents "snap into action immediately—they rent out my room"); the bad marriage joke ("My marriage, or, as it was known, the Ox Bow Incident"); the take my wife! joke (his wife's rape "was not a moving violation"); the sexually overeager joke ("When I see a girl that beautiful, I want to cry or write a poem or jump on her!"). In good Borscht Belt tradition, he had a rabbi who confused the Ten Commandments with the Seven Dwarfs and, like many an odd-looking comic before him, described himself as "basically a stud." In Nichols's words, Woody was now preoccupied with "fill[ing] from within"; later he'd have time to "comment from without." Allen told the *Saturday Evening Post:*

> All good comedians . . . are men we relate to. America is involved in the life of Jack Benny and Bob Hope. Put them in any standard comic situation— say, a roomful of pretty girls—and you know how they're going to react.
>
> If people come away relating to me as a person, rather than just enjoying my jokes; if they come away wanting to hear me again, no matter what I might talk about, then I'm succeeding.

To reiterate, stand-up comic Woody "as a person" is a smart, alienated, human little Jewish analysand at odds with a cold, mechanized urban world. His audience, "the people who must come away wanting to hear me again," is a warm exception to the rule of universal indifference bordering on malevolence, the sympathetic analyst to his wacky neurotic.

The relationship Woody establishes with his audience in the nightclub acts is one he'll use and build on throughout his career. In an early routine, he describes an argument he's had with the government over how to deduct psychiatric expenses from his tax bill. Though Woody says they're a business expense, the government insists they're entertainment: "We compromised finally and made it a religious contribution." And following a similar logic, Woody addresses us, his paying "psychiatrist" (who might also be considered business or entertainment), with mock reverence. In a typical opening remark— such as, "Since I was here last, a lot of significant things have occurred in my private life that I think we could go over tonight and evaluate . . ."—he pleads for compassion, but never presumes equality; since we are obviously comelier, less neurotic, and certainly luckier by the accident of not being in his shoes. And while it wins a laugh, the diffident analysand pose has more insidious purposes besides. The isolation of the stand-up comic is, after all, an awesome handicap. And while the comic's traditional response has been to fight back with wisecracks and swaggering, Woody makes a virtue of his innate shyness, proclaiming his vulnerability in unctuous disclaimers, confessions, and well-charted stammers—the idea being, who could attack such a creature? The distinctiveness of this pose has narrative benefits as well. So much of Allen's art is a roller coaster ride through his fertile imagination, and we need something to cling onto during the journey; that something is Woody himself.

And still Woody can often prove a false friend, his protested fragility—look at me, how neurotic and ungainly and Jewish I am!—serving as a smokescreen for incisive judgments of others and of life itself. The Park Avenue doorman routine is a transparent example. On its subjective (Woody) level, this is the story of a hopeless loser who's not even safe in a "rich and secure and expensive and great" Park Avenue apartment because his doorman assaults him. But from an objective point of view, what sort of world is this if even Park Avenue doormen can't be trusted? So what at first seems a self-parodic tale of personal insecurity is also a comment on the insecurity of the modern world.

Challenging life with the one hand, waving the truce flag of his own inadequacies with the other, Allen's strategy is that of the fool who flourishes a grinning moppet likeness of himself while insulting the king in *Everything You Always Wanted to Know about Sex.* And though he's not the first performer who, while seeming to peer at himself, turns a mirror to the world, few since Chaplin have so persuasively played with our sympathies. Like that earlier tramp—and in contrast to Sahl and Bruce—Woody Allen is less urgently compelled by social, political, or even metaphorical realities than by the idiosyncracies of his own nature. It is not "modern alienation" or "social injustice" but Woody himself who stands at the center of Allen's most profound work. Thus, what we feel about Woody is thematically vital. And thus it follows that when Allen in *Stardust Memories* (like Chaplin in his equally unpopular *Monsieur Verdoux*) dares to create an unsympathetic, even an offensive persona in order to drive home a point, that point is not an indictment of others, but of himself.

But young stand-up comic Allen had no such intentions in

mind. His early routines are short, self-effacing, and dedicated to letting us know who he is so we can like him. Much of Allen's early material focuses on Woody's bad luck: parents whose values are "God and carpeting"; a grandfather who was "a very insignificant man. At his funeral, his hearse followed the other cars." Woody's pet, purchased at the "damaged pet shop," was a dog that stuttered B-b-b-b-bow-wow. (The robot dog in *Sleeper* is a variation on this "damaged pet.") According to another routine, Woody's parents bought him an ant and told him it was a dog. He believed them, of course, until the night the ant failed to pounce on the neighborhood bully . . .

Woody also inherits traits from favorite comedians. Like Bob Hope, he's a surly coward who, when attacked in his lobby, "very quickly lapsed into the old Navajo Indian trick—of screaming and begging." When he and his friend Eggs Benedict both get "pains in the chestal area," Woody displays Jack Benny's emblematic cheapness and lets Eggs pay for the diagnosis. And Woody's frailty recalls both Chaplin and Hope. In the mode of Chaplin, he's so physically vulnerable, the big guys —kidnappers, germs, "Neanderthals," even doormen—can't resist him. Yet, more in the manner of Hope, he coaxes them on: by wearing a white sheet in the deep South, by insulting the pugilistic Hemingway, or getting into cars with strangers.

The difference between the exuberant ironies of the club acts and early films and the grim ironies of the later work often boils down to a matter of emphasis. Where *Manhattan* and *Stardust Memories* will underplay Woody's uniqueness—his funny looks, his social awkwardness—in order to convey the tragic universality of his predicament, the monologues *dwell* on Woody's singularities to comically distance him from ourselves. The club acts' use of another inherited distinction, Woody's Jewishness, is a case in point. Woody was married by a Reform rabbi—"very Reform, a Nazi," and his wife specialized in German recipes, such as "chicken Himmler." In one routine, a "real dyed-in-the-wool Madison Avenue advertising agency" hires him:

> . . . to prove to the outside world that they would
> hire minority groups. I was the one they hired, you

know. I was the show Jew of the agency. I tried to
look Jewish desperately. Used to read my memos
from right to left all the time. They fired me finally
'cause I took off too many Jewish holidays.

Significantly, Allen's Jew is not only a social victim, but
sometimes an undeserving winner or, by implication, an exploiter like son Woody who goes to work for his father and
"organized a union and drove him out of business." Often, like
most of us, he's victim and exploiter at once. In "The Vodka
Ad," for instance, a prestigious vodka company asks Woody to
advertise their product. (They discovered his name in Eich-
mann's pocket.) He says, no, he doesn't drink vodka, and if he
did it wouldn't be their label. "Too bad," muses the vodka man,
"it pays $50,000." "Hold on, I'll put Mr. Allen on the phone,"
says Woody.

Now Woody is really in a quandary because he's "working
on a nonfiction version of the Warren Report," and he needs
the money. So he consults with his "spiritual counselor," his
rabbi, who insists that "it's illegal and immoral to advertise a
product you don't use just for the money," and Woody sadly
rejects the offer. The next thing he knows his rabbi is staring
at him from the pages of *Life* magazine, "with a cool vodka in
his hand."

Allen's cynicism comes cloaked in yet another singularity in
"Mechanical Objects." "I have never in my life had a good
relationship with mechanical objects of any sort—anything I
can't reason with or kiss or fondle," Woody announces. His
clock runs counter-clockwise. His toaster "pops up my toast
and shakes it and burns it." He hates his shower because "if I'm
taking a shower and anyone in America uses his water, that's
it for me. I leap from the tub, scalded."

One night Woody calls "a meeting of my possessions . . . I
said, 'I know what's going on, and cut it out.'" Two nights
later, the portable television misbehaves, and he clobbers it.
He's riding an elevator the next day, "and the elevator says to
me, 'Are you the guy who hit the television?'" The upshot of
the tale is that Woody's bad luck with machines is yet another
family trait. That night he learns that his father was fired:

He was technologically unemployed. My father
worked for the same firm for twelve years. They
fired him, they replaced him with a tiny gadget
. . . It does everything my father does, only much
better. The depressing thing is my mother ran out
and bought one.

Very early in his nightclub career, Allen began addressing
himself to two of the day's major issues, politics and sex. As
contemporary reporters repeatedly observed, Allen's political
repertoire was uncharacteristically slight for a sixties comedian;
and his only sustained political piece—a PBS special dedicated
to spoofing the Nixon administration—was unfortunately never
aired. (After screening the special for a private audience in
Washington, PBS was pressured into canceling the program.)
In *On Being Funny,* Eric Lax has reprinted Allen's original
script, which gives a fair account of Allen's attitude toward
governments, then and now. In one section of the script, a
narrator announces, "Nixon appoints his former law partner
John Mitchell as Attorney General. Mitchell has many ideas
for strengthening the country's law enforcement methods and
is hampered only by lack of funds and the Constitution." Later
the relationship between "Harvey Wallinger" (obviously Kissinger) and Nixon is described as "a personal relationship as well
. . . If you want something done, you have to be in good with
Harvey. If Mrs. Nixon wants to kiss her husband, she has to
kiss Harvey first."

As these few examples suggest, Allen's political routines are
among his silliest and least pointed. He really couldn't care less
about Kissinger or Mitchell or Pat Nixon, or George Washington and Karl Marx for that matter. Political figures and events
simply don't capture his imagination, and if what he has to say
about them is not especially kind, it is not especially heated
either. There's none of the wistful cynicism which characterizes
the love and morality routines here, and little of the specificity.
When Woody describes an "enormously liberal girl" as having
"pierced ears and black clothes and very involved with herself,"
for instance, the person he has in mind need not be an anti-war
marcher: she could as easily be espousing the "fashionable"
cause of est or yoga.

Allen's sex routines and "the wife" gags, on the other hand, are a good deal more specific, pointed, and often abrasive. Here the Kugelmass dilemma of magic versus reality is unambiguously spelled out, with magic as the woman Woody doesn't possess—the stewardesses "running amok" in his bachelor apartment, and prosaic reality as the wife he has and places "under a pedestal."

Of course, in some cases the sexism is only superficial. In one routine, for instance, Woody relives the herculean accomplishment of getting his date into bed, and then confides, "We're making love . . . In an effort to prolong the moment of ecstasy . . . I think of baseball players." And while his conquest approach is off-putting, the inspired juxtaposition of "ecstasy" and "I think of baseball players" goes way beyond the all-male game of "scoring" to capture the tug of war between mind and body, magic and glands which is the arduous mystery of sex for men _and_ women. Still, from a 1980s viewpoint, many of these sex and "the wife" anecdotes rankle; and Vivian Gornick brings an interesting interpretation to them—and to the impact of cultural assumptions on art—in a _Village Voice_ article written nearly a decade after she first saw the nightclub acts.

> What was most striking about Allen's humor in those years is that this Jewish anxiety at the center of his wit touched something alive in America at that moment, and went out beyond us . . . It made Jews of gentiles, it made women identify with his myopic, dishevelled attempts at sexual success . . . It meshed so perfectly with the deepest undercurrents of feeling in the national life that it made outsiders of us all.

Yet, by the early seventies, Gornick "found myself identifying with the foil rather than the comic . . . And God knows I could no longer find his ridiculing pursuit of women _funny_. The deep unspoken references vibrating in each of us at any given point in cultural time and from which all art—comic or otherwise—takes its life, no longer had wholeness or focus for me in Woody Allen's movies."

Gornick's remarks are sharp and revealing, but equally

revealing (and of something quite different) is her disappointed, almost angry tone. For if our response to Woody
varies with changing times and values, the fundamental nature of that response is timeless. As Richard Schickel
confirms when he asserts that for a whole generation,
"Woody, c'est moi," Woody demands passionate identification. He is not the comic who evokes the foibles of our family
and friends, but who represents "in extremis" our own deepest hopes and fears. Furthermore, Gornick's observations suggest the precarious nature of Woody's intensely personal
humor. For when he doesn't faithfully represent our own impulses (innate or culturally determined), when he deviates
from "moi," we feel betrayed.

While contemporary accounts dwell on Woody's anxiety,
shyness, and pain, tapes of his acts suggest a wide range of
attitudinal poses. There's the mock cocky approach of the
"I'm a stud" routines, for example, and the mock hard-nosed
detective delivery that characterizes the kidnapping and sci-fi
acts. Most inventive is Woody's interweaving of whimsical
and streetwise tones in his longer, usually later routines
where, having established his identity, he experiments with
style and a wider variety of source material. On a performance level, routines like "Down South," "The Great
Renaldo," and "The Moose" are masterful exercises in modu-
lation. More important, they anticipate Allen's mature work
in their deft jugglings of multiple themes and their swift shifts
in point of view.

One of the earliest of these long routines, "Down South," is
visually evocative as well. We can almost *see* Woody, dressed
as a ghost, en route to a costume party in the deep South:

> And a car pulls up, and three guys in white sheets
> say, "get in." So I figure it's guys going to the party
> as ghosts. And I get into the car, and I see they're
> not going to the party, and I tell them. And all of
> a sudden it hits me—down South, white sheets,
> Grand Dragon. I put two and two together, and I
> figure there's a guy going to the party, dressed as a
> dragon.

Comprehension dawns too late, and the Ku Klux Klan prepares to hang Jewish Woody:

> And suddenly my whole life passed before my eyes. I saw myself as a kid . . . swimmin' at the swimmin' hole and fishin' and fryin' up a mess o' catfish; goin' down to the general store and gettin a piece a' gingham for Emmie Lou. And I realize it's not *my* life!

Moments later, he's talked the Klan out of hanging him: "I was really eloquent. I said, 'Fellas, this country can't survive unless we love one another regardless of race, creed, or color—and they were so moved by my words that, not only did they cut me down and let me go, but that night I sold them $2,000 worth of Israel bonds."

It is in routines like "Down South" that Allen's magic versus reality conflict finds playful voice. Here magic is the man in the ghost costume, while reality is the Ku Klux Klansman. Magic is Woody's daydream remembrances of "swimmin' at the swimmin' hole," which are not *his* real life; while reality is the fact of being a Jew surrounded by bloodthirsty anti-Semites. And the comic miracle is that magic wins out—Woody's words are so "eloquent" they transform these bigots into supporters of Israel.

In "The Great Renaldo," one of the best of these longer routines, the reality versus magic conflict boils down to a battle between Woody's senses (responding to real life) and his fertile imagination (susceptible to magic). When the monologue begins, Woody is all reality: a tired New Yorker sitting quietly at home on a Sunday evening, watching "The Ed Sullivan Show." (The time is the late sixties.) One of tonight's guests is a hypnotist, who entrances a volunteer from the audience and tells him he's a red fire engine. At this point Woody falls asleep, and when he awakens he's "suddenly . . . seized with an uncontrollable desire to dress up in my red flannel underwear. I burst out the front door and start running down Fifth Avenue, making siren noises . . ."

So far the monologue has been "realistic": no matter how outrageous the image (or action) he perceives, Woody describes it in concrete terms. But now, and to the delight of the audience, magic makes its entrance, and Woody's "hypnotized" voice tells us he meets another hypnotized comrade, and "we decide to work as one truck." And thus the battle begins: one moment Woody talks as a man in red pajamas, the next as a fire engine; now he's regaling us with extravagant flights of fancy, now catching us up with unexpected plunges into common sense. As with most of the early films and plays, as well as the club acts, the competition is close, but magic triumphs in the final seconds. A policeman comes to round up the Woody who starts "giggling hysterically." Because he's been brought down to earth at last? No, because "this guy's trying to get a fire engine into a lousy little Chevy."

The most intricate of Allen's nightclub routines is his 1965 "The Moose." Structurally, this act is a kind of detective puzzle, with its three clues—the moose, the law, and the Jew—deftly embedded in the narrative. The trick, as we not so quickly perceive, is for Woody to turn the clues into as many crimes as possible—each one building on the last, and each increasingly inventive. Our job is to try to anticipate where he's headed—or, more to the point, just keep up.

"The Moose" opens with Woody's most unlikely crime: "I shot a moose once. I was hunting in upstate New York, and I strapped him onto the fender of my car." As it happens, the moose isn't dead, only "creased." So Woody finds himself driving home through the Holland Tunnel with a live moose on his fender. "And the moose is signalling for a turn, you know. And there's a law in New York State against driving with a live moose on your fender, Tuesday, Thursday, and Saturday."

Thus far, the routine is a spiral of vividly described incongruities. There's the visual absurdity of a moose waving paw signals at Manhattan traffic and the personality incongruity of Woody, the passive New Yorker, venturing past city limits, much less *hunting* upstate. And doesn't the government think of everything? Even an absurdly irrelevant rule for moose-carriers.

Plot and thematic implications thicken when Woody resolves to escort the moose to the Solomon's costume party to "ditch

him . . . It won't be my responsibility," "it" referring to both
the moose his date and the moose his crime. At midnight the
moose suffers a Pirandellian blow when costume awards are
handed out, and he comes in second to the Berkowitzes, "a
married couple dressed as a moose." So here we get our second
crime and an inkling of what Woody is up to thematically. This
must be a routine about reality being less real than art; or maybe
about the wrong people getting rewarded.

And yes, it is, in a way. But Woody's already ahead of us,
reshuffling his clues. The moose, furious at losing first prize, is
"locking antlers" with the Berkowitzes. Then the moose is
forgotten, and Woody "is driving along with two Jewish people
on my fender. And there's a law in New York state . . . Tuesday,
Thursday, and especially Saturday." Here's the third crime,
and the second inkling of a theme. Is this the Madison Avenue
advertising agency again? Is Woody saying that moose-carriers
(and other citizens) are afflicted by absurd regulations mas-
querading as government or religion? Yes, but . . .

The next morning, when Mr. Berkowitz wakes up, he's been
"shot, stuffed, and mounted at the New York Athletic Club.
And the joke is on them, 'cause it's restricted!"

A great pleasure in all Allen's work is its deceptive simplicity.
Although scheme of "The Moose" is complex, Woody's approach is so conversational a child could follow it. Like the best
of artists and athletes, he makes his craft look easy. He gives
the impression of prevaricating, of making random comments
and extraneous allusions. His unfinished or reiterated phrases
convey the spontaneity of a Second City improvisation. The
first time Woody mentions the New York State law for moose
drivers for instance, it seems a throw-away remark. We're too
absorbed with the idea of a half-dead moose straddling Woody
Allen's fender to give the bureaucrats in Albany much thought.
Yet that "throw-away," like the apparently irrelevant fact that
the married moose couple is Jewish, is Allen's lead to his punch
line incongruity: that the New York Athletic Club's "laws" ban
Jews, but the members proudly (though unknowingly) display
a Jew-in-moose's-clothing. And while its tone is exuberantly
comic, "The Moose" has serious points to make: that magic
(the costumed Berkowitz "moose") is more persuasive than

reality (the "real" moose); that restrictions by and against a particular group are similarly absurd.

The development of Allen's nightclub art anticipates the development of his four other careers. In each case, he begins with carefully selected models and works to make them his own. Both in their style and their content, the early club routines are consciously indebted to Hope, Sahl, Youngman, and Nichols and May; while "The Great Renaldo" and "The Moose" have seamlessly assimilated these influences. And although the influences are important, at the core of Allen's work is an original vision.

In his parable of the hedgehog and the fox, Isaiah Berlin says, "The hedgehog knows one big thing," and so, in a sense, does Allen, though he has varied, redefined, and rendered it more and less palatable over the years. The "biggest" thing Allen knows, and has known since "The Great Renaldo" and "The Moose," has to do with the incongruities within and between individuals, society, and life itself: between concept and action, art and life, person and pose, substance and style, etc. At the end of *Catch-22*, Joseph Heller's idealist, Major Danby, tells the pragmatic Yossarian that he must not look at people, but "up at the big picture" because "ideals are good, but people are sometimes not so good." To which Yossarian rejoins, "When I look up, I see people cashing in. I don't see heaven or saints or angels. I see people cashing in on every decent impulse and every human tragedy." And so does Allen—in a way. But, on the other hand, when he sees people cashing in, he also sees heaven and saints and angels. When he sees the moose on the wall of the New York City Athletic Club, he will always remember the Berkowitzes.

=3=

Wanderer
in Chinatown

Getting Even,   What's New, Pussycat?
Casino Royale,   What's Up, Tiger Lily?,
Don't Drink the Water,
Play It Again, Sam (play),
The Woody Allen Television Special

In *Stardust Memories,* protagonist Sandy Bates is obsessed with the metaphysical absurdity of things. Life is two parallel trains —the one carrying the beautiful, the other, the grotesque people —both of which wind up in the same desolate junkyard. It's the search for the perfect woman you don't believe exists, and the fact of having achieved fame, fortune, and the clout to do precisely what you want, but still being miserable and unde- cided. Reality and the dilemma of choice are too much with Sandy. Or, as a younger Allen prototype might have sized up the situation, "Can we actually 'know' the universe? My God, it's hard enough finding your way around Chinatown."

In the mid-sixties, Woody Allen was more like the wanderer in Chinatown than Sandy Bates in existential depression. As Allen has been telling us for years, life is as much a matter of pesky as of momentous absurdities. And the moral question need not involve "heaven and saints and angels." It may be whether or not to make the vodka ad: which, in fact, Allen did make. Similarly, fantasy need not be Sandy Bates's twin exalted illusions of death and artistic excellence. It might be: You are a stand-up comic with a growing, though modest reputation. One night a major film producer comes to see your act and, two days later, has contracted you to write and play a starring role

in a big Hollywood comedy. It's a daydream come real. Well
—in a variation on the Ku Klux Klan memory routine—it's not
your daydream; but why not? Or you're offered a television
special, a cover story article in *Esquire,* the chance to be master
of ceremonies on the "Tonight Show," when only a few years
earlier you were a lowly comic writer.

For Allen, the mid to late sixties were a time of consolidation
and uncertainty. He forged a lasting relationship with managers
Jack Rollins and Charles H. Joffe, who remain his agents,
producers, and trusted friends to this day. He married and
separated from Louise Lasser, who also remains a close friend.
He travelled to Europe to make *What's New, Pussycat?* and
Casino Royale for producer Charles Feldman. And he sat in his
study dreaming up personal projects or studying comic play
and essay models.

Professionally, Allen's reality in the sixties was that of the
young artist experimenting with opportunities born of his growing success. By 1965, a happy confluence of personality, performance, and comic art had made him a well-known stand-up
comic, but he wanted to move beyond the nightclub format.
Story- and playwriting were longtime ambitions; mainstream
comic journalism, scriptwriting, and television were now also
viable options. Yet Allen's problem, as he branched into different areas, was how? Which gifts should he stress? The persona's
claims on the creator became a career as well as an artistic
tension. For Allen had developed a comic persona whose
broader qualities—alienated schlemiel with delusions of "scoring"—could be translated into essays, cartoons, films, and
plays, offending few and amusing large commercial audiences.
But he had also touched a deep nerve of intelligent social anxiety and alienation and, in routines like "The Moose," had
evolved an art whose subtlety and intellectual range would not
appeal to everyone.

It's too simple to portray Woody the crowd-pleaser schlemiel
in battle with Allen the serious artist. In one of his better works
of this period, *Play It Again, Sam,* Woody and Allen are as
felicitously, if not as provocatively, mated as in the nightclub
acts. Yet, for the most part, the essays, plays, and scripts of this
era are not as strong as the club acts. And frequently the
grinning moppet face of Woody does obscure Allen's art.

This is certainly the case in a 1969 _Life_ cover story which is representative of one of the two distinct sorts of essays Allen wrote during the period. Entitled "How Bogart Made Me the Superb Lover I Am Today," this essay is a mock confessional "key" to the genesis of _Play It Again, Sam._ Its opening swiftly establishes the narrator as broadly self-parodic early Woody. The first Humphrey Bogart film he saw was _The Maltese Falcon:_ "I was ten years old, and I identified immediately with Peter Lorre. The impulse to be a snivelling, effeminate, greasy little weasel appealed to me enormously . . ." When he reached puberty, however, "my sex glands suddenly [made] their debut like a Boston socialite and my interests [turned] rapidly from the sinister to the romantic." After a first disappointment in love, narrator Woody returns to _The Maltese Falcon,_ and this time "I didn't identify with Peter Lorre. My heart went directly to the master and I was hooked for life."

Soon "I was walking like Bogart, talking like Bogart, curling my lip and saying, 'No thanks, sweetheart. Oh, you're good. You're really good. Play it again, Sam.' I know he never actually said, 'Play it again, Sam,' but I said it enough for both of us."

Then, Woody falls "head over McCarthy button in love with Lou Ann," an ideal he meets "at a freak-out in Greenwich Village (I was freaking in at the time due to a bad sense of direction)." They spend three months together, after which she runs off with a drummer in the rock group "The Concluding Unscientific Postscript" and he returns to _The Maltese Falcon._ He loves the film as much as ever, but now concludes, "The only safe thing is to identify with the actual falcon itself. After all, it's the stuff dreams are made of."

"How Bogart Made Me the Superb Lover I Am Today" is indicative of the mainstream comic essay Allen frequently contributed to national magazines like _Life_ and _Esquire_ during the late sixties. Characteristically, it reiterates Woody's idiosyncrasies and suggests, without truly probing, a conflict between life as it is and life as it could be. Daydream identification with Bogart leads Woody to romantic love; disappointment in romantic love heads him to art (the falcon). Certainly, there's the germ of an idea here, but it's overwhelmed by the facetious tone and by overemphasis on Woody's foibles.

Getting Even

The other and invariably deeper sort of essay Allen composed during this period does without the Woody persona altogether and aims to perfect the fine art of S.J. Perelmanesque comic prose. Compiled in Allen's first literary collection, *Getting Even,* pieces like "The Gossage-Varbedian Papers" and "The Metterling Lists" first appeared in *The New Yorker* and small literary magazines in the mid-sixties. And while his mainstream comic writing petered out in the early seventies, the more specialized *Getting Even* stories mark the beginning of a fruitful, if peripheral, career which has persisted over the past two decades and brought us *Without Feathers* and, most recently, *Side Effects.*

As Allen is first to admit, *Getting Even*'s indebtedness to Robert Benchley and especially S.J. Perelman is great. Indicative is a comparison between the openings of Perelman's "Somewhere a Roscoe" and Allen's "A Little Louder, Please." Writes Perelman:

> This is the story of a mind that found itself. About two years ago I was moody, discontented, restless, almost a character in a Russian novel. I used to lie on my bed for days drinking tea out of a glass. (I was one of the first in this country to drink tea out of a glass; at that time fashionable people drank from their cupped hands.) Underneath I was still a lively, fun-loving American boy who liked nothing better than to fish with a bent pin. In short, I had become a remarkable combination of Raskolnikov and Mark Tidd.

Writes Allen:

> Understand you are dealing with a man who knocked off *Finnegans Wake* on the roller coaster at Coney Island, penetrating the abstruse Joycean arcana with ease, despite enough violent lurching to shake loose my silver fillings. Understand that I am among the select few who spotted instantly in the

Museum of Modern Art's impacted Buick that pre-
cise interplay of nuance and shading that Odilon
Redon could have achieved had he forsaken the delicate ambiguity of pastels and worked with a car
press.

A shared entangling of reason and lunacy, substance and
pose, the esoteric and the colloquial, reveals a basic affinity
between Allen and Perelman which goes beyond style to a
comic impulse Allen describes as "hostile," a perception of life
as inherently chaotic. Where the club routines borrow specific
traits and attitudes from Hope or Sahl or Nichols and May,
Perelman's influence on the essays is more diffuse. Beneath
fustian poses, the *Getting Even* narrators, like Perelman's, are
often unredeemably mean-spirited, and the world they inhabit
is at once less awesome and more niggardly than the nightclub
world. Where Woody is thwarted by a cruel universe, the Perelman and *Getting Even* narrators are pettily outsmarted by their
own small tricks.

And yet *Getting Even* is also intimately related to the club
acts of this period. As in the acts, the subject matter varies:
"The Metterling Lists" parodies abstruse scholarship; the short
play "Death Knocks" at once spoofs and pays homage to Ingmar Bergman's *The Seventh Seal.* But here too the central
thematic conflicts are between magic or illusion and reality,
between life as "heaven and saints and angels" and as "people
cashing in."

Indeed, some of the best of the *Getting Even* pieces are of the
"Not only is there no God, but try getting a plumber on the
weekends" variety, dedicated to putting the lofty in pragmatic
perspective. Like Sandy Bates in *Stardust Memories,* these stories envision life in terms of parallel trains. Along one track run
beauty and truth; along the other, ugliness and treachery.
There's one train of thought for concepts like God and Metterling's art and Mafia crime, another for routine necessities like
the plumber and Metterling's laundry list and Mafia office sup-
plies.

A typical *Getting Even* parody involves a collision of parallel
thought processes. An idea starts out at the plumber's and
winds up in the heavens or, as is more frequently the case, an

idea starts out in God's country and plunges earthward. In the essay "Spring Bulletin," for instance, the narrator describes a course entitled "Philosophy XXIX-B" as "Introduction to God. Confrontation with the creator of the universe through informal lectures and field trips." Or an abstraction may be brought down a peg or two, as in the same narrator's description of "Rapid Reading":

> This course will increase reading speed a little each day until the end of the term, by which time the student will be required to read *The Brothers Karamazov* in fifteen minutes. The method is to scan the page and eliminate everything except pronouns from one's field of vision. Soon the pronouns are eliminated. Gradually the student is encouraged to nap. A frog is dissected. Spring comes. People marry and die. Pinkerton does not return.

Here the *idea* of reading more books is doubly undercut: first, by the *means*—take the easy way, take a course!—and then by the narrator's use of language. As in the club routines, we laugh not only because what we're told is absurd, but also because that absurdity is so close to what passes for reason all around us. The prospect of reducing a whole book to "Pinkerton does not return" is funny in itself, but funnier still when one considers the goals of exercise machines, microwave ovens, and, yes, rapid reading courses. And how cleverly Allen suggests these absurdities—dramatizing the rapid reading method ("reducing" his own sentences from a lengthy first to a cryptic last) even as he satirizes the concept.

As "Rapid Reading" demonstrates, a major difference between the club acts and the *Getting Even* essays is the difference between the sympathetic Woody, who suffers from whatever travesty Allen describes, and the essay narrator, who is invariably part of that problem. If the travesty is self-serving commitment, for instance, the narrator will be more hypocritical than Tartuffe; if the hard-boiled detective is Allen's target, his narrator will overplay the Hammett pose; or if Allen is out to skewer the venal scholar, his narrator's voice is that of "The Metterling Lists," which opens:

Venal & Sons has at last published the long-awaited
first volume of Metterling's laundry lists . . . with an
erudite commentary by the noted Metterling scholar
Gunther Eisenbud. The decision to publish this
work separately, before the completion of the im-
mense four-volume "oeuvre," is both welcome and
intelligent, for this obdurate and sparkling book will
instantly lay to rest the unpleasant rumors that
Venal & Sons, having reaped rich rewards from the
Metterling novels, plays, and notebooks, diaries and
letters, was merely in search of continued profits
from the same lode. How wrong the whisperers have
been! Indeed the very first Metterling laundry list

List No. 1

6 prs. shorts
4 undershirts
6 prs. blue socks
4 blue shirts
2 white shirts
6 handkerchiefs
No Starch

serves as perfect, near-total introduction to this
troubled genius, known to his contemporaries as the
"Prague Weirdo."

And so continues "The Metterling Lists," with the Freudian
slip serving as catalyst for ever more outrageous collisions of
style *and* ideas. Every time Allen's mincing pedant of a narrator starts to trumpet the purity of his endeavor, he seemingly
can't stop himself from revealing all his petty motives. When
he succeeds in emitting an "erudite" (albeit meaningless) adjec-
tive, he's bound to soon follow it up with a derisive noun like
"lode." And in case the reader should still harbor any illusions
about the nature of the material this man has painstakingly
collected, see List No. 1.

While the humor of "The Metterling Lists" is unambiguously denigratory, a piece like the short play "Death Knocks"
conveys slightly more complex feelings. A spoof of Ingmar
Bergman's ultra-solemn *The Seventh Seal,* (one of Allen's favorite films), the play opens as Death, a "schlep" variation on

Bergman's hooded stranger, pays a middle-of-the-night call on fifty-seven-year-old dress manufacturer Nat Ackerman. Where Bergman's knight protagonist suggests a game of chess for his life, Ackerman and "his" Death play gin rummy. And Allen's partly self-parodic point (one which will be provocatively explored elsewhere) is clear from the outset: man creates Death —and, by implication, all abstractions—in his own image. Bergman's knight gets a brilliant, articulate chess champion; Allen's dress manufacturer gets a whining middle-aged Jew who can't even win at gin. (On the other hand, while the knight dies, Allen's unworthy manages to survive.) "Death Knocks" is filled with broadly comic dialogues, such as one where Death uses Nat-like reasoning to establish his identity:

> *Nat:*   Who are you?
> *Death:* Death. You got a glass of water?
> *Nat:*   Death? What do you mean?
> *Death:* What's wrong with you? You see the black
>   costume and the whitened face?
> *Nat:*   Yeh.
> *Death:* Is it Halloween?
> *Nat:*   No.
> *Death:* Then I'm Death . . .

What "Death Knocks" does for the Grim Reaper and Bergman's *The Seventh Seal,* "Mr. Big" does for God and Dashiell Hammett's *The Maltese Falcon.* Like the club act "The Moose," "Mr. Big" is constructed as an allegorical puzzle; the components here are religion, the hard-boiled detective story, and existential philosophy. The narrator is Kaiser (a parody of Hammett's tough shamus), the missing person, God. As the story opens, a "dame" asks Kaiser to track down "the creator, the underlying principle, the First cause of things, the All-Encompassing." Kaiser is not enthusiastic, but because the "dame's" figure "could cause cardiac arrest in a yak," he agrees to do his best. The routine sources are approached: Rabbi Wiseman, for instance, who scoffs at the idea that he might have seen "Him" lately. "Are you kidding?" he wonders. "I'm lucky I get to see my grandchildren." Chicago Phil tips Kaiser off: "There's nothing out there. It's a void. I couldn't pass all those

bad checks or screw society the way I do if for a second I was
able to recognize an authentic sense of being."

As in "The Metterling Lists," the narrator's language as well
as his thought process is subject to bouts of disassociation. God
gets mixed up with Delancey Street, Kierkegaard is discussed
in the same breath as the Mafia. There's a message to this
strange convolution: that the shamus approach to the mystery
of God is no more or less absurd than the approach of organized
religion, or of existential philosophy, for that matter. And this
message is wittily conveyed in a conversation between Kaiser
and a police sergeant on the "death" of God:

> He was dead when they brought Him in.
> Where'd you find him?
> A warehouse on Delancey Street.
> Any clues?
> It's the work of an existentialist. We're sure of that.
> How can you tell?
> Haphazard way how it was done. Doesn't seem to
> be any system followed. Impulse.

Where "Death Knocks" and "Mr. Big" observe the disparity
between the "big" metaphysical concept and the little mind that
perceives it, "A Look at Organized Crime" and "Viva Vargas"
contrast the awesome or terrifying institution with its very
human membership. Often Allen's point is only the familiar one
that even Homer nods, but it's cleverly articulated. "A Look at
Organized Crime," for instance, describes the duties of a Mafia
chief as: "Meetings are held at his house, and he is responsible
for supplying the cold cuts and ice cubes." "Viva Vargas" also
has food on its mind. Taking a short view of the glorious
revolution, its rebel cook narrator sighs: "The situation has
taken a turn for the worse. As luck would have it, the mushrooms I so carefully picked to vary the menu with turned out
to be poisonous . . ."

Where the *Getting Even* essays' "big absurdities" connect to
the themes of the nightclub acts and, indeed, of all Allen's
deepest work, their narrators display the sort of petty contradictions of character that will be stressed in Allen's early
dramas. The *Getting Even* narrator may be a rebel cook or a

pedant or a hard-boiled existentialist. But whoever he is, he is absurd, and absurd on an individual rather than an abstract level. Confronted with the terrible contradictions of life, the *Getting Even* narrator is not unlike Woody's parents in the nightclub routine who, upon learning that their son's been kidnapped, "snap into action immediately—they rent out my room." The Allen narrator copes by looking out for Number One, by taking the short and narrow view, by escaping into pretense (to wisdom, stature, sex appeal, whatever quality he clearly doesn't possess): in other words, by deluding himself and (usually unsuccessfully) scheming to delude others.

In his *Getting Even* context, this character conveys Allen's serious message that (to quote T.S. Eliot) "humankind cannot bear very much reality." But Allen soon discovered that, as with the persona, this sort of character need not be anchored to a *Getting Even* context or even to the essay medium. Just as Woody's foibles are resonantly funny in the club acts and frivolously so in the *Life* piece, the *Getting Even* narrators' eccentricities can seem profound or silly, depending on the situation Allen invents.

And in the mid-sixties Allen began inventing dramatic as well as literary situations, embedding the distinguishing traits of Woody and/or the *Getting Even* narrators into such film and play characters as scheming Felix of *What's New, Pussycat?* myopic Walter Hollander of *Don't Drink the Water,* and neurotic divorcé Allen of *Play It Again, Sam.* As Allen remembers this era, "I was always interested in writing for the theater, but films were something I got sidetracked into." In 1964 producer Charles Feldman asked Allen to write and co-star in what would become *What's New, Pussycat?,* and seeing no reason he shouldn't, Allen agreed. Two years later, while waiting out shooting delays on his second Feldman movie, *Casino Royale,* Allen wrote his first full-length play, *Don't Drink the Water.*

As with his essays, Allen's dramatic work during the sixties falls roughly into two camps. On the one hand, there is his hired-hand scriptwriting, where financial rewards were great and creative freedom minimal. His films reached large audiences—*What's New, Pussycat?,* for instance, became the highest-grossing comedy to its date, but at the cost, very great for an intensely personal artist such as Allen, of ultimate control over his material. Allen's two sixties plays, on the other hand, reached smaller audiences and reaped less staggering financial profits. But here he enjoyed the playwright's prerogative of relative artistic control.

Yet, in both arenas, Allen was similarly limited by his status as beginner. Like the typical *Getting Even* narrator, he had to juggle what he wanted to do with what he could get away with; he had to weigh his ultimate dramatic career goals against the immediate need of surviving in the highly competitive world of show business. "You tend to stay with what you can do, just out of a sense of survival," Allen recalls of this era. "I felt that if I wanted to stay in show business, in plays and films, I could always, as my father would say, make a nice living out of comedy. But at the same time I longed to write serious drama."

This tension between Allen's comic and serious impulses is more keenly felt in the early plays. With the film scripts, he was low man on the collective totem pole, straining to make even his lightly comic voice heard above the din of producers, directors, and stars. *What's New, Pussycat?* was an especially exasperating experience. As least powerful of three collaborators, Allen was continually bowing to Feldman's and director Clive Donner's anticipations of a bawdy sexual farce with glamorous women and exotic settings. "There's a big difference between what you want to do with a script and what gets done," Allen wryly observes. And whatever his original intentions were, *What's New, Pussycat?* is a broad, episodic comedy which, in its best moments, exploits the characters and situations of Allen's stronger work.

The lead character of Michael (Peter O'Toole), for instance, recalls the more conventional and/or attractive foil for Woody in the nightclub acts. An expatriate reporter in Paris, Michael is one of three men whose love dilemmas are the subject of the film. His particular dilemma—the most unusual for early Allen —is that "when the light falls on me in a certain way," all the women in the film want to go to bed with him, and he with them. And he's frustrated if he doesn't but guilty if he does because he's in love with one woman, Carol (Romy Schneider), who wants marriage and fidelity.

Caught between flesh and spirit, Michael turns to psychiatrist Felix Fassbender (Peter Sellers), who, with pressing love problems of his own, "can't take more than fifteen minutes of [Michael's] love life at one time." A cross between ungainly Woody with illusions of "studliness" and an intellectually pretentious *Getting Even* narrator, Felix despises the wife who dotes on him and lusts after the female patients who find him repulsive.

Victor's (Woody's) love dilemma is that of early Woody: lusting after all women, loved by none, and in love with his best friend Michael's fiancé, Carol. Like Woody in the club routine, he's had too much experience with a particular kind of oral contraception: "The girl said 'no.' " Yet Allen gives him a friendly, whimsical quality; and, atypically, Victor is the one character not involved in any sort of psychotherapy.

Just as "How Bogart Made Me the Superb Lover I Am Today" touches on conflicts between magic and reality, *What's New, Pussycat?* alludes to the exasperatingly different needs of mind and body which are explored in Allen's deepest work. As in *Love and Death* and *Manhattan,* most everyone here is in love with someone who prefers someone else; and, with romantic pariah Victor as exception, each is troubled by the unwanted attention of yet another. So love has no external logic. Nor has it internal congruence: Michael is monogamously in love with Carol, but promiscuously in lust with half of Paris. And Carol likes Victor, who suits her standards of fidelity, but loves Michael, who doesn't. And to further complicate matters, *What's New, Pussycat?* is itself romantically incongruent, for its central love story has two contradictory resolutions. On the one hand, Michael does marry Carol, but on the other, he is already flirting with new "pussycats." As with the upcoming *Bananas, Sleeper,* and *Manhattan,* the lovers may or may not end up living faithfully ever after.

What's New, Pussycat? is weakest in its (many) sexual chase scenes and best when it focuses on Felix and Victor. As with the narrators of "The Metterling Lists" and "Hassidic Tales," Felix's detached, professional pose readily accedes to unprofessional inclinations, usually of a sexual order. And he inevitably confuses his role as psychiatrist with his psychological needs. Thus, he greets his wife with the primal scream, "I hate you!" and conducts his group therapy sessions like a private dating service.

Victor's foibles too are imaginatively conveyed. His cowardice is revealed in a library sequence where he can't summon up the nerve to defend Carol's book from an aggressive reader. His lechery is suggested by his job—as "dresser" for strip-tease dancers—and stressed in a café scene where Michael inquires about his wages:

> *Victor:*   20 francs.
> *Michael:* That's not very much.
> *Victor:*   It's all I can afford.

Where most of *What's New, Pussycat's* plot is gag-oriented, there's one sequence which subtly conveys the illusion/reality tension. Set on a deserted bank of the Seine, this scene is a confrontation between celebrating Victor and suicidal Felix. While the former fastidiously sets his solitary birthday table, the latter prepares to kill himself. Real-life romantic disappointments are too much for both Victor and Felix. But while Victor copes by figuratively drowning his sorrows in birthday champagne, Felix literally wants to drown himself in the river. The trouble is that Victor simply won't let Felix die in peace. So, after an initial spat, the two dreamers—in a sense, two sides of the Allen persona—get to chatting and exchanging hard-luck stories and absurdly impractical romantic tips. (Felix, for instance, assures Victor that his woman troubles will be over if he buys a sports car.) And each goes back to Paris happier and no more enlightened for their meeting.

The personal and professional frustrations Allen experienced during the making of *What's New, Pussycat?* were repeated, on a smaller scale, with *Casino Royale* and *What's Up, Tiger Lily?*: both spoofs of the James Bond genre film. Again, Allen was given credit without creative control. For Feldman's *Casino Royale* he (purportedly) created the cameo role of Jimmy Bond, an impish, sexually jealous nephew to the great James. And he was billed as director, actor, and screenwriter on *What's Up, Tiger Lily?*, a Japanese thriller with a dubbed English soundtrack.

"These are not my films," Allen says, emphatically. "I was responsible for only one scene in *Casino Royale*—the execution scene, and that I ad-libbed. And I hated *What's Up, Tiger Lily?*

and sued to keep it from coming out. Other writers were
brought in to add stupid jokes. Even my voice was dubbed—
at times by another actor!"

Allen's chagrin is understandable, as *Casino Royale* and
What's Up, Tiger Lily? are extremely flawed works. While
What's Up, Tiger Lily? is the livelier of the two, both films
overemphasize the one-joke incongruity between suave, in-
trepid Bond and cowardly, gauche Woody. *What's Up, Tiger
Lily?* is a gag-after-gag collision between Japanese thriller images and Woodyish dialogue. The Japanese hero, for instance,
is addressed as Phil Moskowitz, and the violent quest we watch
is described as a search for the perfect egg salad recipe. Some
of the collisions are inspiredly silly. During a *visually* intense
sequence between a bearded man and a man with a mustache,
for instance, we *hear:* "Don't interrupt . . . or I'll have my
mustache eat your beard." And as Phil appears about to crack
the safe that holds the precious recipe, a female voice announces
that she's going to the ladies' room. May she bring another girl
with her? The movie continues in this juxtaposing fashion to a
split-screen finale: with China Lee stripping on one side and a
printed disclaimer running down the other.

Parodies such as this are best in small doses, and brevity is,
indeed, a virtue in Allen's scenes in *Casino Royale.* His character, Jimmy Bond, makes two very short appearances. In the first
(which Allen ad-libbed), he outwits his would-be firing squad
by tossing a hand grenade. (This sequence will be more tragically varied at the end of *Love and Death.*) In the second (which
Allen didn't script), he plays the neurotic New Yorker to
"Uncle" James's (David Niven's) composed Englishman. As
Jimmy squirms, pouts, and congratulates himself on outwitting
his uncle, James clucks, "All this trouble to make up for your
sexual inadequacy" or "I'm just beginning to see that you're a
trifle neurotic."

Whatever their shortcomings, Allen's sixties scripts are a
solid beginning. Even at their most pedestrian they possess the
component Preston Sturges described as essential to comic
writing—the two- as opposed to the one-liner, the comic dialogue. But what they conspicuously lack is the structure to
forge that dialogue into a cohesive narrative and thematic statement. Were Allen truly an anarchic artist, this formlessness

might be a statement in itself. But Allen is most provocative when his anarchic spirit is forced to contend with a tight dramatic structure. And it's the presence of this structure which distinguishes the still lightly comic *Don't Drink the Water* from Allen's sixties film work. For beginning with this first play, and continuing throughout his theater and much of his film career, Allen weds his unique imagination to specific, often traditional dramatic models: in this case, to George S. Kaufman and Moss Hart's classic 1936 Broadway comedy *You Can't Take It With You* and John Patrick's successful 1953 *Teahouse of the August Moon.*

In keeping with both these plays, *Don't Drink the Water*'s plot is a matter of parochial, set-in-their-values Americans being forced into close quarters with freer spirits, American and otherwise. The dramatic tension derives from a clash of values and temperaments; the resolution from a recognition of shared —though very different—illusions and, more to the practical point, of a common enemy.

Don't Drink the Water's parochials are New Jersey caterer Walter Hollander, his wife, Marion, and their less narrow-minded daughter, Susan. Its eccentrics are the assorted inhabitants of an American embassy "somewhere behind the Iron Curtain." The two camps meet when unwilling tourist Walter ("thirty-five hundred dollars for three weeks of uninterrupted diarrhea") innocently snaps a picture in what turns out to be a Communist missile zone, and the secret police chase the Hollanders into the arms of the American embassy. The rest of the play becomes an attempt to get the Hollanders home.

As in *Teahouse of the August Moon,* each of the parochials has an obsession (or obsessions) as eccentric as the eccentrics' idiosyncrasies: entrepreneurial Walter, for instance, is obsessed with the idea of getting home to his catering business; fastidious Marion is obsessed with cleaning; even realistic Susan is obsessively prone to falling in love with eccentric losers. And if *Don't Drink the Water* has a message, it is that a hick is a hick. Or, otherwise phrased, that a person of limited imagination (such as Nat Ackerman in "Death Knocks") unfortunately can't appreciate the unfamiliar opportunity—here a European holiday—but fortunately can't comprehend an unfamiliar terror, like being trapped behind the Iron Curtain, either. The Hollanders' obsessions, variations on Woody's daydreams in the club acts, keep them from appreciating their *real* danger; and, paradoxically, because they don't appreciate the danger, they survive it.

Most of the *Don't Drink the Water* characters are interesting variations on the *Getting Even* and nightclub figures. Walter Hollander—a role Allen wrote specifically for Lou Jacobi—is part Nat Ackerman and part Woody's shortsightedly cunning father. Father Drobney, the play's narrator, combines Woody's illusions with the *Getting Even* hypocritical pose. As well as an ineffectual priest, Drobney is Allen's first literal magician. But, significantly, he's a failed magician, as incapable of extricating himself from his magic straitjacket as from real-life troubles. The play opens with Drobney's description of those troubles:

> Six years ago I ran [into the United States embassy] seeking asylum from the Communist police. Outside these walls were four million Communists determined to kill me! My choice was simple. I could remain here in the safety of your embassy, or I could go outside and attempt the biggest mass conversion in history. I decided to stay. . . .

Drobney proceeds to introduce us to Ambassador Magee, off on a political mission to the United States; to Magee's upwardly mobile assistant Kilroy; and to Axel Magee, in Drobney's words: "Not exactly bright-eyed, not exactly efficient, in fact the only man in the history of the foreign service to accidentally wrap his lunch in a peace treaty . . . This man has worked at this embassy for six months. That's the longest he's ever worked at any one embassy. Why? Because he's pleasant, he's eager, and he's the ambassador's son."

Appointed acting ambassador in his father's absence, Axel displays most of Woody's gaucheries and insecurities but little of his redeeming intelligence. A would-be career diplomat, he has the distinction of having upset domestic as well as international relations in his first seventeen posts. His father grimly notes: "You were in Brazil for two weeks, and you had them importing coffee!" And while he has no difficulty recognizing an attractive woman, such as Susan, when she comes his way, kissing her is a major production that involves tripping, crawling, and upsetting most of the props on stage.

Again as with Woody, the world has always been too importunately against Axel. And the thrust of the play is toward his taking arms, both romantically—with Susan—and practically, by coming up with the idea that will get the Hollanders out of Eastern Europe. Predictably, the former is easier than the latter. Axel's first escape plan for the Hollanders—in which they would be exchanged for a "brilliant" Communist spy—is inconveniently foiled when that spy hangs himself in a Berkeley jail. His second scheme involves elaborate false identifications and guns and is equally futile. Ultimately, Axel does spirit the Hollanders home, dressed as Arab nobility, but not until everyone has had a chance to display his true colors under pressure. Until xenophobic Walter has addressed a very important Arab sultan, "What's your trouble, Alladin?" Until incorrigibly ingenuous Axel has told the Communist Chief of Police, "Look—you spy on us—we spy on you . . . Why do we suddenly pretend it's unusual?" and convinced him that the Hollanders are spies. Until the two-faced Kilroy (apparently unctuous, but in fact scheming to usurp Axel's position) gets hit in the head and begins thinking like *both* the Wright brothers: "Come quickly, Wilbur. I'm coming, Orville. I'm telling you, Wilbur, we can do it. Do what? Get those machines to fly. Orville, you're crazy . . ."

Anticipating most of Allen's later work, *Don't Drink the Water* operates on both a real and a fantastic level. On the fantastic level, Allen has caricatures attending to business as usual under highly unusual circumstances. On the level of reality, he has those circumstances: an American family vulnerable to the whims of a Communist secret police. The character link between fantasy and reality is Susan, who, but for her unrealistic love for Axel, is the embodiment of common sense.

Like most of the *Getting Even* essays—and in contrast to both "The Moose" and the upcoming *Play It Again, Sam*—*Don't Drink the Water* is *emotionally* real only when it's fantastic. That Marion should confront the threat of imminent death just as she confronts the threat of dust in her New Jersey house makes perfect emotional, if not much practical, sense. It's like Woody's parents renting out his room when they learn he's been kidnapped. It's like the "Viva Vargas" rebel cook picking (poisoned) mushrooms to vary the troops' menu. They do what they can. We suspend our disbelief about characters like Marion and Walter and Father Drobney at their most fantastic because, at their most fantastic, they merely take our own predilections an absurd step further. As many a Roman can attest, when in Rome, we're less likely to do as the Romans than to do what went over well at home. Walter the hostage behaving like Walter the caterer is a universal truth in comic extreme, a funny abstraction.

Unfortunately, Walter the real character is only a mannequin over which Allen drapes that abstraction, and thus the emotional scenes between himself and Marion, and between Axel and Susan, are the least effective. Susan is especially problematical. Though she's a necessary bridge between the absurd characters and their *real* problem, her dialogue is flat, and she stands out like a sit-com character in the midst of a farce. (In *Play It Again, Sam,* Allen will solve this problem by making his pragmatic straight man, Dick Christie, so obsessive that he seems just as eccentric as the dreamers.)

Don't Drink the Water, which opened at Broadway's Morosco Theater in 1966, was an important work for Allen. As would be true of all his plays, it was better received by audiences than by critics. While Lou Jacobi's performance was acclaimed, *The Wall Street Journal* was indicative in deeming the play itself "fine for gag lovers, but not quite so fine for those who expect comedies to have some structure." But the structure, though simple, is there, and Allen's central idea of provincialism on holiday is firmly rooted in character and theme. Furthermore, while *Don't Drink the Water*'s form is derivative, its tone is distinctly Allen's, as is the double twist to the illusion/ reality contest at the end of the play when unrealistic Axel, inspired by love for realistic Susan, comes up with the idea— his first of a lifetime—which gets everyone home.

Play It Again, Sam

Where *Don't Drink the Water* is a solid dramatic beginning, the 1969 *Play It Again, Sam* is an accomplished work which brings to a close and, in a sense, together most all of Allen's sixties beginnings. Though never so thematically dense as "The Moose" or "Mr. Big," this second play unites the persona and the deep humor of the club routines and *Getting Even* essays within a tight dramatic structure learned from *Don't Drink the Water.* Even the Feldman movies are obliquely involved. Acting in *What's New, Pussycat?* and *Casino Royale* gave Allen the confidence to write the leading role in *Play It Again, Sam* for himself.

Play It Again, Sam looks to the future as well. As in *Don't Drink the Water,* Allen acknowledges a dramatic model—this time *The Seven Year Itch*—but, by stressing conflicts between illusion and reality, Allen here makes the model more assuredly his own. His character relations now take on a real as well as a surreal life; and, more important, in the original Broadway production, Allen acts with Diane Keaton and Tony Roberts for the first time. The compatible rhythms and ineffable chemistry of this team are *Play It Again, Sam*'s crucial legacy to Allen's future art and will be explored in a later analysis of the Herbert Ross movie. And yet, as Dudley Moore's long run as lead in the London production confirms, *Play It Again, Sam* has distinct, if modest, virtues of its own.

This play is to Allen's second divorce (from Louise Lasser) what the "wife" routines are to his first, although it's not strictly autobiographical. "What did occur [in real life]," Allen told Lax, "is that married friends would say, 'Oh, we know a nice girl for you.' They'd introduce me to a girl and it would be an awkward evening . . . and I'd make a fool of myself frequently. Then I would find that the wives of my friends, who I wouldn't in a million years think of being lovers with, I'd be natural around them and real."

When *Play It Again, Sam* opens, twenty-nine-year-old Allan Felix, writer for a small New York movie magazine, is suffering from the simultaneous defections of his wife Nancy and his analyst. Of the latter, he remarks: "If only I knew where my damn analyst was vacationing. Where do they go every August? They leave the city. Every summer New York is full of people who are crazy till Labor Day." Allan is crazy because his wife of two years has left on a definitive note: ". . . I can't stand the marriage. I don't find you fun. I feel you suffocate me. I don't feel any rapport with you, and I don't dig you physically. For

God's sake don't take it personal!'' Yet, like the persona, Allan responds schizophrenically—resigned to inevitable loss one moment, he's scheming to win Nancy back the next.

Also in keeping with Woody, Allan inhabits the intersecting worlds of fantasy and reality. And anticipating *Love and Death*'s Boris (who, at "the happiest time of my life," experiences suicide pangs), Allan is as inclined to escape from a kind as from a wounding reality. Thus, during the play's early scenes, when reality is grim, Allan takes refuge in Humphrey Bogart movies or soothing daydreams. But when life promises to live up to his wildest fantasies, when beautiful Linda Christie falls in love with him, Allan all the more compulsively escapes into nightmare visions of retribution.

But in the early scenes, fantasy and reality episodes are evenly balanced. In his fantasy life, Allan often confers with Humphrey Bogart, who, like Nat Ackerman confronted by Death, perceives Allan's romantic predicament within the limits of his own experience. "Dames are simple," he swaggers. "I never met one who didn't understand a slap in the mouth or a slug from a forty-five." Oblivious to Allan's tetchy relationship with liquor, he prescribes drowning thoughts of Nancy in "a little bourbon and soda." In real life, Allan pops aspirin, sucks up TV dinners, and wonders how his analyst could have suspected a sexual problem: "Isn't that silly? How could there be a sexual problem? We weren't even having relations." He also begins seeing a lot of Linda Christie.

There's a twist to the fantasy-reality contest in *Play It Again, Sam* in that Allan's fantasy companion, Bogart, shares only his small body and "kinda ugly" looks, whereas his real life friend, Linda, is as neurotic and illusion (daydream and romance)-prone as he. Linda is the wife of Allan's best friend, Dick Christie, who, as the play gets underway, is determined to get his morose friend back on the dating track. Like Bogart, aggressive businessman Dick appraises Allan's problem in his own language: "A man makes an investment—it doesn't pay off." The thrust of the play is toward finding Allan a better deal.

Play It Again, Sam is so carefully constructed that when Allen wanted to revise it for a movie version, he found he could neither add nor delete a single incident. More than with *Don't Drink the Water*, a seemingly casual dialogue in one scene resonates in the next. In Allen's memory sequence, for instance, Nancy lists a few apparently arbitrary complaints. She wants to go "discothequing and skiing . . . You like movies because you're one of life's great watchers. I'm not like that . . . I want to laugh." But these specific complaints pay off in the following scene when Allen reconstructs them for Linda. "Insufficient laughter, that's grounds for divorce. And skiing. She wants to ski down a mountain, laughing like an idiot." Similarly, Allan's fantasy identification with Bogart in the first act pays off in his own *Casablanca*-like gesture in the last.

Although its triangular love story is familiar, *Play It Again, Sam*'s characters are sensitively developed. A model for most of the later Diane Keaton roles, Linda Christie has little but sexual reticence in common with the "enormously liberal" Bennington graduates who reject Woody in the club routines, and she shares few of Susan Hollander's realistic traits. Like Bing Crosby to Bob Hope, Linda's as much Allan's alter ego as his foil. Though more conventionally attractive and socially assured, she's as imaginative, emotionally vulnerable, and essentially insecure as he. And Linda's as needful of Allan's birthday presents and sincere compliments as he is of her mothering: for while Nancy has *physically* vanished, business-preoccupied Dick has left Linda emotionally unsupported. The neurotic rapport between Linda and Allan is established in an early scene in which she asks for an aspirin.

> *Allan:* I ate all the aspirins. What about Darvon?
> *Linda:* That's okay. My analyst once suggested Darvon when I had migraines.
> *Allan:* I used to get migraines, but my analyst cured me. Now I get tremendous cold sores.
> *Linda:* I still do. Big ugly ones—from tension.
> *Allan:* I don't think analysis can help me. I may need a lobotomy.
> *Dick:* The two of you should get married and move into a hospital.

Although he displays Axel Magee's judgment (he buys quicksand in Florida and radioactive lots in Tennessee), Dick Christie is *Play It Again, Sam*'s answer to straight man Susan

Hollander. Like Susan, Dick is practical. But in contrast to Susan, Dick's pragmatism is unpragmatically excessive. Some of the play's best gags revolve around his obsessive, self-locating calls to a business answering service. In an early "real life" episode, he tells his service, "Hello, this is Mr. Christie. I'm leaving the Gramercy number now and proceeding due north to the Murray Hill number." Later, in Allan's imagination, Dick comes to inform him: "I've fallen in love with . . . an Eskimo . . . Well, I'm off to Alaska. If you need me I'll be at Frozen Tundra 7-0659." And one of the play's narrative incongruities is that Dick's best friend and wife should fall in love before his unseeing "pragmatic" eyes.

For his part, Allan Felix is a less brilliant, more human variation on stand-up comic Woody. Like Woody, Allan is anxious, smart, maladroit, eager to "score," and emotionally discriminating. Partially because he tries too hard—overswathing himself in after-shave, posing as a Renaissance man, "pouncing" prematurely—Allan alienates every woman he pursues. Vanessa the nymphomaniac is eager to hop into bed with anyone but him; Gina the Catholic conveniently forgets to take her pill; the "fantastic little blonde" in the discotheque "erupts into derisive laughter" at the sight of Allan dancing. When Allan tries to score in an art museum, the Bohemian object of his desire is "committing suicide" and thus not free on Saturday night.

So, on the one hand, Allan's failures are pathetic, but, on the other hand, they're well earned. For like the persona in the Las Vegas mirror seduction routine, Allan is so narcissistically bent on scoring he barely notices the women involved. Secretly, he looks down on these rejecting creatures. "I'm fussy," he tells Linda. "I don't know how I can afford to be, but I am." And, paradoxically, we find his scheming, male-chauvinistic indifference reassuring, because the truly pathetic character—such as Paul in Allen's next but much later play, *The Floating Lightbulb*—is painful to watch.

Allen's second play is a decade and comic worlds away from his third. The most conventionally optimistic of his dramatic works, *Play It Again, Sam* creates not only a protagonist as sinning as sinned against, but three central characters whose problems are superficial and thus easily resolved. Dick's neglect of Linda, for instance, is only a passing mood. He tells Allan,

"If I haven't already lost her to someone, I'm going to make up for everything . . . I'm going to change. I'm going to do everything I can to make her life with me exciting and fun because without her it wouldn't be worth living." Similarly, Allan's incompetence is merely the neurotic "stud" pose he assumes with strangers. As Linda assures him, "You have a lot going for you. You're bright and funny and even romantic, if you could only believe it. You put on a false mask as soon as you meet a girl . . . I keep telling you . . . be yourself. The girl will fall in love with you."

And so, as romantic convention warrants, by the middle of the second act, Linda has fallen in love with Allan and he with her. In Dick's absence, they plan an innocent dinner which, first in Allan's fantasy and then in real life, winds up in the bedroom. Predictably, the scoring is not easy. A shouting match with the imagined Bogart, a smashed lamp (by Linda), and awkward compliments (by Allan) like, "Linda, your eyes are like two thick steaks," must be endured before the worlds of friendship and love successfully collide. And fantasy-reality, friend-lover, concept-execution collisions pursue Allan and Linda throughout their "brief encounter." As Allan remembers the sequence of events, he "took [Linda] into my arms and we made love. Then we both got upset stomachs." In order to perform sexually, he—like "Woody"—thinks of baseball players. And, after the fact, he suffers movie-inculcated fantasies of Dick's return. In a daydream melodrama, Dick verbally reprimands:

> How could you? My wife and my best friend. I trusted you both. I feel I've been made such a fool of. I loved her. I loved you. Why didn't I see it coming? Me—who had the foresight to buy Polaroid at eight and a half.

In an Italian film fantasy, cuckolded Dick brandishes a dagger.

Characteristically, Allen's fantasies and moral instincts dim the prospect of romance with Dick's wife. So, again characteristically, moments after Linda's called the affair off ("I don't regret one second of what's happened because what it's done for me is to reaffirm my feelings for Dick"), Allan sacrifices real-life love for friendship and romantic fantasy:

> *Allan:* [Dick] came by while you were out. He
> wants you to go back to Cleveland with
> him . . . Meanwhile, we'll just be good
> friends . . . I think I'd like that . . . You're
> part of his work, the thing that keeps him
> going. If that plane leaves the ground and
> you're not with him, you'll regret it . . .
> *Linda:* That's beautiful.
> *Allan:* It's from *Casablanca.* I waited my whole
> life to say it.

For all its thematic resonances, the final message of *Play It Again, Sam* is unambiguously summed up in Allan's parting words with Bogart:

> *Bogart:* You don't need me anymore. There's
> nothing I can show you you don't already
> know.
> *Allan:* I guess that's right. The secret's not being
> you, it's being me. True, you're not too tall
> and kinda ugly. But I'm short enough and
> ugly enough to succeed by myself.

In contrast to "The Great Renaldo" and "The Moose," *Play It Again, Sam* ends with a bow to reality and a hint of the sixties "just be yourself and the world will love you" bromide besides. Of course, there are ironic nuances to Allan's *Casablanca*-like sacrifice of Linda, for the reality he chooses over romance is the opportunity to live out his fantasy of playing Bogart. And he sacrifices love, not only to friendship and fantasy, but also, one suspects, to his vision of the (for him) unhappy rightness of things. Still, the play's denouement is unqualifiedly sanguine. After Bogart leaves Allan's apartment, a young movie afi-cionado, Barbara, wanders in to use his phone. Like Linda—and in contrast to the nymphomaniacal Vanessas and "fabulous little blondes" of the world—Barbara is impressed with Allan for what he is: to her, a film scholar. "You're not *the* Allan Felix who writes for *Film Quarterly,* are you?" she wonders. Indeed he is, and as the curtain falls, Allan's expostulating on his favorite topic of Bogart, and the girl is raptly attentive. Thus the romance of soul mates begins afresh, and—in a variation on

Allen's concluding observation in "How Bogart Made Me the Superb Lover I Am Today"—the "only safe thing" is to *use* your fantasies to real life advantage.

If *Play It Again, Sam*'s uncharacteristic optimism befits the culminating work of a decade which, for Allen, saw so many endeavors well-begun, the play itself is indicative of yet another conflict in Allen's art. For while *Play It Again, Sam* is well wrought and often affecting, its artistic success is not commensurate to that of the later club routines and *Getting Even* essays. Although it draws upon the autobiographical associations of the nightclub acts—notably for its persona-like protagonist, "Allan"— it is never so complex and innovative as the nightclub work. Woody's quicksilver shifts in mood and sly intelligence are missing in the more predictable Allan. And the raw comic energy and multiple style/theme convolutions of both the acts and the essays find no answering voice in the more amiable longer work.

As Allen moves from the sixties into the seventies, he confronts a conflict between natural talents and ambitions. Born of a yearning for excellence and a need to continually move beyond what has already been done well, this conflict will profoundly influence Allen's work in the coming decade. Its implications are suggested in a comparison between *Play It Again, Sam* and a CBS Woody Allen special, produced in the same year and also dedicated to displaying Allen's varied talents to a wide commercial audience. But here similarities end: for where *Play It Again, Sam* forces those talents into a sustained dramatic work, the special presents them in short sketches, monologues, and interviews. And while *Play It Again, Sam* is, for Allen, the more challenging work, the special—and notably a short film called "Cupid's Shaft," a Billy Graham interview, and a *Pygmalion* spoof—is fresher and more insightful.

In "Cupid's Shaft," for instance, Allen deftly intermingles parody of Chaplin's *City Lights* with self-referential parody and social satire. Co-star Candice Bergen plays a rich young woman with amnesia (Allen's answer to Chaplin's blind girl) who, "her mind gone . . . wanders dazed to the rotten section of town." There she meets paper collector Woody, a pathetic and menacing (he lances one bench-sitter's newspaper) young wastrel.

Wealthy, beautiful girl and repulsive, impoverished man fall in love and vow to marry. But the girl's memory—and sanity—return. And, in Allen's more biting interpretation of the Chaplin story, she flees to the wealthier arms of another, leaving despondent Woody to stab papers alone, now in the rain.

Merging Charlie with Woody, eloquence with gutter talk, satire with homage, "Cupid's Shaft" is the Allen incongruity in top form. His interview with Billy Graham is similarly felicitous. The built-in joke here is, of course, the fact of Graham the true believer turning up on Woody the skeptic's television special. But Allen pushes for subtler incongruities, suggesting, through manner and word, that his conflict with Graham the symbol need not preclude affection for Graham the person. A skilled interviewer, he establishes an atmosphere conducive to friendly jousting. Indicative is a discussion of their respective convictions. When Graham invites Woody to a revival meeting, the latter replies:

> *Woody:*   You could probably convert me because I'm a push-over . . . You know what I mean . . . I have no convictions in any direction. And if you make it appealing enough and you promise me some wonderful afterlife with a white robe and wings . . . I could go for it.
>
> *Graham:* I can't promise you wings . . . but I can promise you a wonderful, exciting life.
>
> *Woody:*   One wing?

From the Graham interview, the special moves into its final and best segment, a *Pygmalion* parody, with Candice Bergen playing baker's daughter Liza to Woody's quack rabbi of a Higgins. Dim-witted and beautiful, the Bergen character longs to be one of the "smart, cultured people who always have something to say. I'm tired of going into museums just to use the bathroom." So her father brings her to a very old, learned rabbi (Woody) who promises, within three months, to pass her off as "one of the country's leading pseudo-intellectuals" at the "annual Norman Mailer Cocktail Party." Meanwhile, teacher and unpromising pupil fall in love. And, after her successful unveiling (thanks to comments like *"Elvira Madigan* was beautiful to look at, but visually it was very uninteresting"), he confesses he's neither scholarly nor old. "And so it came to pass," comments the narrator, "that two people of different worlds got married and lived together in mutual harmony—until the divorce . . ."

Far from routine network fare, these special segments are scrupulously crafted and, what's more, quite adventurous, presuming audience knowledge and tolerance of Chaplin, Shaw, atheists, and divorce. Allen's religious references are especially daring: a rabbi who's unflatteringly old, ugly, and insincere; a "One wing?" perception of the afterlife, comparable to the "enormously liberal girl's" (fashionable) vision of politics. And where *Play It Again, Sam* leaves marriage and friendships intact, the "Pygmalion" sketch foils expectations of "happily ever after" with a last sentence divorce.

But beyond specific irreverences, all these special sketches display Allen's comic gifts to their best advantage. There's an exuberant sagacity here that is not felt in the tamer and more tentative *Play It Again, Sam*. And since both the play and the special are so-called commercial ventures, the difference in quality is not a matter of accessible versus specialized humor, but of a sustained versus a fragmented structural format. The greater success of the special, as of the nightclub routines and the *Getting Even* essays, suggests that the piece—the short essay, the club act, the dramatic sketch—rather than the whole is the natural vehicle for Allen's talents. What is more difficult for him is the sustained work; and more difficult still is the sustained work which combines the acuity of the special with sympathetically drawn characters, such as Allan Felix and Linda Christie.

Allen goes into the seventies more provocatively conflicted than he was in the mid-sixties. His parallel trains have, so to speak, multiplied. The moral and career and comic versus serious choices are now compounded by a fundamental artistic tension between his gift as a comic sketch writer and his goal of creating sustained drama. He is now a well-known, even—like Napoleon—a "famous person," but he's also, more pressingly, an artist determined to experiment and change.

=4=

A New Track

Take the Money and Run, Bananas,
Play It Again, Sam (movie),
Everything You Always Wanted to Know
About Sex* (*but were afraid to ask)

The keen visual talent suggested by Allen's longer nightclub routines is memorably displayed in his first feature films. Food for the South American rebels (in *Bananas*) is an image of 1,500 little green take-out bags and coleslaw "to go" in wheelbarrows. Prison escape (in *Take the Money and Run*) is a shot of convict Virgil Starkwell whittling a bar of soap into the shape of a gun and blackening it with shoe polish. And preparing to "score" (in *Everything You Always Wanted to Know About Sex*) is a spaceship of sperm wading through fettucini and waiting for the take-off signal. The pause between comic sketches is a blink of the camera. And our guide is still a small, redheaded, bespectacled young man, now in his early thirties, who buys the deli take-outs, whittles the gun, and is ejected with the rest of the sperm—but his imagination may well be elsewhere.

Although film is the medium through which Allen will probe his deepest themes and subtlest contradictions, his film career begins in the dense but playful spirit of "The Great Renaldo." Magic conflicts with reality in most every surreal frame of his first three films, but the consequence is usually preposterous, as is the context: Woody as crook and social enigma in *Take the Money and Run*, as machine demonstrator and South American president in *Bananas*, or respectively, as medieval fool,

Italian husband, sex researcher, and sperm, in his four sections in *Everything You Always Wanted to Know About Sex*. And these films are audacious in the manner of the early Woody persona, rather than Allen, for while they impishly attack other peoples' "fantasies" of social and political solutions, they rarely grapple with issues whose ambiguities trouble the artist himself.

During the sixties, Allen branched out. During the early seventies, he begins concentrating his energies on a sort of filmmaking which has little to do with the Feldman scripts or *What's Up, Tiger Lily?* and a lot to do with searching for a bridge between the raw energy of the nightclub acts and the dramatic unity of *Play It Again, Sam*. While he continues writing short essays and one-act plays, Allen will not write another full-length play for over a decade and, in the early seventies, will give up mainstream journalism, scriptwriting, and finally his nightclub performing. By 1972, he will have directed three feature films and discovered, in the film medium, a natural outlet for his unusual gifts.

Just as Allen's early plays are derivative of Kaufman and Patrick, his stories of Perelman and Benchley, *Take the Money and Run, Bananas,* and *Everything You Always Wanted to Know About Sex* rely heavily on the comic film tradition. As Allen himself notes: "In *Bananas,* I train for the army the way Abbot and Costello do in their films or the way Bob Hope does in *Caught in the Draft*. The jokes are different, but the basic structure is conservative." And he also recalls that in these first, as opposed to his later, films, he "got more of a personal kick out of just being funny," which comes across in the inspired lunacy of the gags, the goofy look of the film and television parodies, and the giddy comic pacing, which becomes a style in itself.

Whether failed crook or unwilling South American president, the early film persona is a smart daydreamer whose inability to function conventionally in real life has driven Jewish parents to near madness—to wearing Grouch Marx masks in *Take the Money and Run,* to contemplating their son's *not* becoming a doctor and inheriting the hospital in *Bananas*. Though he hasn't a stutter, the Woody character in these early films is as objectively pathetic as young Paul in *The Floating*

Lightbulb, with the difference that he's broadly, comically malicious besides. He burrows his head in a porno magazine while the woman beside him gets mugged, and directs a parking car back, back, back until it crashes into another vehicle. And like Bob Hope, the early Woody physically overstates: twirls ballet circles in glee, swaggers in anticipation of scoring, and squirms and screws up his face at the prospect of pain. Like Sandy Bates in a very different context, Virgil Starkwell and Fielding Mellish challenge our affections. But in contrast to both Sandy and Paul, they have perfect comic faith in the efficacy of their most ludicrous illusions, which take them out of the realm of despair and into crime, revolution, and, a bit more successfully, romantic love.

As in the club routines, connections between Woody and Allen run deep. The slapdash look of *Take the Money and Run* and *Bananas,* like the "um" and "well ahs" that pepper the acts, are less a function of novice craftmanship than of artist posing as persona. Allen's skewed camera and haphazard pacing are the stylistic equivalent of Virgil's botched prison escapes and Fielding's ungainly "pouncing." Once again, this pose is a self-effacing gesture to the audience. Don't be awed that I've made this film, it intimates. This was a stroke of luck, rather like Fielding's winning the girl at the end of *Bananas.* And if it happened to me, it could more easily happen to you.

The priorities Allen establishes with these first features will also characterize later career choices. After *Take the Money and Run,* he signed a contract with United Artists which provided for unusually low budgets—two million dollars for each of three features—and extraordinary creative liberties. "I wanted to have complete freedom," he said recently, "and in order to get that freedom, I was willing to make inexpensive films." Since *Take the Money and Run,* Allen has had "a blank check to do what I want. Nobody gets to read the script—I could make my next three films with my mother and father if I chose. And that's very important for someone like myself." Also important for Allen has been a team of loyal crew members. With the exception of executive producers Rollins and Joffe, Allen's early team did change. Dale Hennesy and David Walsh made way for Mel Bourne and Gordon Willis. But the fact of a talented crew with loyalties which endure beyond an individual project remains constant.

A vital crew member on every film through *Annie Hall* is editor Ralph Rosenblum, who helped turn *Take the Money and Run*'s promising but, in Rosenblum's words, "formless" first cut into logically related adventures of Virgil Starkwell (Woody). Rosenblum's account of his first encounter with Allen (published in *When the Shooting Stops*) is revealing. In January 1969, Rosenblum received a worried phone call from Jack Grossberg, production manager on *Take the Money and Run*. Despite Allen's reputation, his first film was so seriously flawed that the distributor, Palomar Pictures, was threatening not to open it. Grossberg wondered whether Rosenblum, known for "saving" such "hopeless" films as *The Night They Raided Minskys*, would agree to work with this famous, shy, intensely private young would-be filmmaker. Rosenblum agreed to look at the film at least, and:

> At nine-thirty on a Monday morning, I arrived at a dilapidated screening room on Forty-third street . . . I soon found myself treated to a very unusual experience, a film that seemed to be flying all over the place, with highs as high as the Marx Brothers and lows as low as a slapped-together home movie . . . The film was packed with funny material. It was frenetic and formless and obviously the work of a very fresh mind. But even as I was enjoying it, I began to feel that it was going on forever. The whole thing was put together in a strange, inept way, with little rhythm and a very bad sense of continuity.

The rough cut of *Take the Money and Run* was also unbearably sentimental at times. There was a scene in the park, for instance, in which escaped prisoner Virgil (Woody) courts the lovely young laundress Louise (Janet Margolin): "The lovers walk up a distant hill with frilly music in the background," recalls Rosenblum, "and something like vaseline on the lens, and the viewer feels as if he's stumbled into another movie." Obviously, the unrelieved romanticism of this scene had nothing to do with the Woody America had come to know and love.

Yet, as Rosenblum wisely perceived, the scene did not have to go: what was needed was a narration to undercut the visual blurriness. Allen quickly appreciated the intelligence of Rosenblum's suggestion and, as would be true throughout their association, ego did not deflect him from following through on his editor's hunch. Thus, in its final cut form, this scene between Virgil and Louise still takes us up the glistening hill, but now with Virgil's voice-over comments in the background: "After fifteen minutes I wanted to marry her, and after a half hour I completely gave up the idea of snatching her purse."

Besides making sure that each of its sketches was true to the spirit of Allen (and not more than Woody, the young persona *and* actor, could handle), Rosenblum made important structural contributions to *Take the Money and Run.* "Since the film was haphazardly plotted, it didn't matter too much where one scene or another ended up," he recalls, "and thus I was able to move things around at will to serve the rhythm and the pace." Still, as Rosenblum is first to admit, most of what became *Take the Money and Run* was present at the primitive, first-cut stage. And at first and last, *Take the Money and Run* is essentially a string of ingenious comic sketches, loosely held together by the familiar presence of Woody and by recurring parodic targets.

Chief among these targets is the cinema-verité "problem" documentary, infused, in the activist sixties, with the assumption that something *can be done:* liberal guilt and government dollars can be mustered to get to the root of the trouble and expunge it. *Take the Money and Run* is Allen's answer to this genre and its fantasy of social betterment. His "problem" here is Virgil Starkwell, an unredeemable and unredeemably incompetent crook; and, along with the ultra-earnest cinema-verité interviews, Allen's means of piercing to the heart of the Virgil problem is to view it from the perspective of old prison and gangster films—notably, *The Defiant Ones, Brute Force,* and *White Heat.* So the social optimism of the documentary clashes with the social cynicism of the gangster genre: need one stipulate which triumphs?

In *Take the Money and Run*'s hilarious opening shot, the portentous voice of Paramount newsreel narrator Jackson Beck confronts the scratchy image of inept Virgil. Reports Beck:

> On December 1, 1930, Mrs. William Starkwell
> ... gives birth to her first and only child. It is a boy,
> and they name it Virgil. He is an exceptionally cute
> baby with a sweet disposition. Before he is 25 years
> old, he will be known to police in six states for
> assault, armed robbery, and possession of a wart.

Meanwhile, we observe the phenomenon of Virgil: as shoe shine boy, spitting past his customer's foot to lubricate a trouser leg; as a petty thief, jamming a gum machine; as incipient victim, standing myopically by as friend and stranger alike stomp on successive pairs of his eyeglasses.

And so *Take the Money and Run* proceeds, picking up ever more outrageous contradictions as it goes: Virgil the social outcast is confronted with Virgil the social threat; the hapless *look* of young Virgil is confronted with the narrator's dire prophesies. No incident in Virgil's life is too trivial for scrutiny. A former cello teacher is unearthed to report, "He had no conception of the instrument. He was blowing into it." A probation officer remembers that "Virgil didn't always tell the truth. Sometimes he exaggerated. Sometimes he just plain lied." Interviewed throughout the film, Virgil's parents face the camera in Groucho Marx masks. Virgil's mother insists that her son was a good boy. "What do you mean, good boy?" scoffs her husband. "If he was a good boy, why are we wearing these masks?" And Louise Lasser makes a cameo appearance as an acquaintance who found Virgil a "nebbish" and "such a nothing" until she learned that a movie was being made of his fascinating criminal record.

Like the *Getting Even* narrators with their literary flourishes, *Take the Money and Run*'s interviewees presume that style—here film style—will transform petty thoughts into profound insights; so they talk on and on in endless banalities. Or else, like Virgil's father, they see the accident of Virgil's notoriety as an opportunity to present their case to a waiting world. "I tried to beat God into him!" wails poor Mr. Starkwell—irrelevantly.

"New" journalism is wonderfully parodied in an interview with the man who photographs Virgil's last arrest. Asked to recreate this momentous event, the photographer (like the

narrator of "Viva Vargas") has trouble getting past his own
stomach: "I was having breakfast . . . two fried eggs, toast, I
can't remember what kind of juice—oh, yes, it was orange juice
. . ." This absurdity is taken a step further when *Take the Money
and Run* itself diverges from subject Virgil to contemplate the
nation at large ("1956 is a happy year for most people"); and
when the camera leaves Virgil's psychiatrist, expatiating on his
former patient, to observe the psychiatrist's current patient,
unattended on the couch.

One of the film's great pleasures is its visual inventiveness. In
keeping with the narrator's many Freudian conjectures, one
early scene confuses the young with the mature Virgil. While
the soundtrack reveals that schoolboy Virgil "is soon good
enough to play (cello) in a local band," Woody approaches,
cello *and* chair in hand, the only cellist in a walking band and
the only thirty-four-year-old in school and, needless to say,
alienated. Virgil's first failed prison break is another example of
visual ingenuity. As previously observed, Virgil whittles a bar
of soap into the shape of a gun and blackens it with shoe polish.
(Dillinger successfully escaped from prison using a similar
strategy, only the gun was wood.) An imaginative conceiver,
Virgil plots real-life escape with a fantasy gun. He has no doubts
that illusion can overcome reality. But, a clumsy executor, he
doesn't prepare for real rain, which turns his hopes to soap
bubbles, and he's back at the drawing board. In a subsequent
Method acting prison break, the prisoners steal the guards'
underwear. ("I'm known for my detail work," brags one convict.) They must *feel* the role in order to fool others.

Take the Money and Run follows Virgil, in vaguely chronological fashion, from unremarkable childhood to unattractive
adolescence to a crime/prison/escape pattern of adult experience. It is during a hiatus between escape and upcoming crime
that Virgil meets the young laundress Louise in the aforemen-
tioned park episode. Thanks to Rosenblum's suggestions, this
scene succeeds in balancing pathos and humor. But, for the
most part, Virgil's relationship with Louise fluctuates between
too-sweet Chaplinesque romance and too-snide marital bickering. Their best scene together, a variation on the many "the
wife" routines in the club acts, takes place on the morning of
an important bank robbery. Though Virgil is late to meet his

pals, Louise refuses to let him use the bathroom first—and is he really going to wear that dreadful shirt to the scene of the crime?

Of the film's two bank robberies, the one becomes a farcical contest between two would-be robber teams, while the other picks up serious implications in the manner of the club act "The Moose." This latter robbery is developed around the anomaly of a timid crook and a belligerent victim. When the scene opens, Virgil is waiting politely on a bank queue. He meekly presents his hold-up note to a teller who, upbraiding him for bad penmanship, forces him to read his note aloud: "Please put $50,000 into this bag and act naturally," he reads and, "I am pointing a gun at you." Still, the teller is suspicious. What Virgil has read as "gun" looks to him like "gub," and he sends Virgil off—head hung low—to obtain the approving signature of an officer. Unfortunately, the officer also has troubles with Virgil's penmanship: "act," as in "act naturally," is, she insists, really "abt." And even after the police have arrested would-be bank robber Virgil, the matter of his "gubs" and "abts" is loudly debated throughout the bank.

Like "The Moose," this bank robbery comically interweaves a number of complex ideas and is outrageously funny because it rings true to mundane experience. The truculent bank teller who can't see past Virgil's artless penmanship to his dastardly purpose is the low-level bureaucrat everywhere—in comic extreme. Like the film's interviewees, he naively presumes that the medium is the message. And, more interestingly, he nearly sways Virgil with this logic. For on one (concept) level, Virgil continues to challenge the law, but on another (action) level, he begins appealing for tolerance. By the middle of this scene adult Virgil is behaving like a whimpering child, and his hold-up note has taken on the properties of a truant boy's letter of excuse from school. So while caricaturing the authority figure, Allen also pokes fun at the "outsider"—the alien, if you will—who challenges the social contract. And while "outsider" Virgil winds up begging for tolerance here, the reverse is true in a later job interview scene in which Virgil begins by accommodating and winds up quizzing his would-be boss.

Though far from a political film, *Take the Money and Run* has its share of politically oriented gags as well. In a chain gang escape episode, a parody of *The Defiant Ones,* collective and individualistic impulses are both wryly dismissed. Social unity is spoofed in a shot of the chain-linked prisoners pedalling down the highway on stolen bikes. (Fittingly, "alien" Virgil is running between bikes, holding up his slack chain like a floor-length gown.) But the ruggedly individualistic sheriff looks no less absurd when he can't recognize these escapees as they literally parade before him, chains clanking. And what of lonesome Louise, so obsessed with her private misery that she can't perceive that her wayward husband has not come home to her by himself? While Virgil sadly informs her, "These men are with me for good," she persists in addressing only her husband.

The chain gang escapade and timid robbery are two of many memorable sequences whose themes resonate throughout *Take the Money and Run,* but whose characters and stories are mostly self-contained. Like the televised special segments, each sequence has a scrupulously crafted beginning, middle and end, but narrative connections between them are desultory, and their arrangement is apparently random. The farcical robbery follows the timid caper, the chain gang escape comes after the soap gun fiasco; but, as neither Virgil nor his relationships substantially grows, the order might as logically be reversed. Unlike Linda Christie, Louise does not demand our sympathies, nor do we much care what becomes of the chain gang or the prisoners in guards' underwear once their sketch is finished.

While *Take the Money and Run*'s virtues far outweigh its shortcomings, certain problems—and, notably, the film's awkward parallels to Chaplin's work—are instructive. A challenge to any filmmaker, Chaplin's personal qualities are especially troubling for a small, alienated, romantic young comic. His genius is an inspiration, of course, but imitation is a problem. And in struggling *not* to imitate, Allen often blunts his own effectiveness. During the love scenes, for instance, Virgil's self-conscious "Chaplin in love" parodies—the rolling eyes, the flailing hands—undermine real sentiment.

More important, this film which so often deals with the concept of alienation never quite comes to terms with the difference between Chaplin and Allen as aliens. Both are little men at odds with a large, cold world, but where Chaplin's enemy is the world at large, Allen's is specifically urban America. And while Chaplin's alienation is a conflict between one man and society, Allen is, in addition, self-conflicted.

This discrepancy becomes evident in *Take the Money and Run*'s "silent film" scene in which Virgil, like so many Chaplin heroes in his position, prepares to court his beloved. Sighing at his manifest inadequacies, Virgil frets about an underfurnished apartment, illogically plucking shoes from his refrigerator, and dressing in the shabby equivalent of Sunday best. His ritual is Charlie's, and yet while Chaplin evokes humor and pathos, Allen can't make this scene work.

And the explanation comes down to words, which Chaplin —with his exquisitely descriptive face and body—has no special need for but which are crucial to Allen's vision of himself and his alienation. For while the tramp is uncomfortable with society, he is gracefully at home within his own body. Woody, on the other hand, is at war with all things physical—his own body included. Woody's sharp intelligence finds no correlative in his droopy, myopic eyes or clumsy legs. Where the tramp strives with all his sorry being against a cruel and perplexing universe *out there,* Woody (in keeping with Allen's mind/body conflict) strives with his brain and humor to succeed despite, not only the universe, but his own red-headed "kinda ugliness." If Chaplin's face is mirror of the man, Woody's is its contradiction. And thus dialogue, which is usually irrelevant to Chaplin's art, is vital to the anomaly of Allen's.

Allen's two endings to *Take the Money and Run* also suggest yet another problem in this early work. His rough-cut ending is not only the more sentimental, it's downright gory. As Allen describes it:

> I died in a most brutal fashion. It was done very realistically. I was wired for bullets, and when I was shot, the plate glass behind me shattered, and I fell to the ground and died, and my leg was twitching . . . My idea was that people would laugh through most of the film, and then at the end—almost as if it were another film—they would get a different sort of experience. But everyone was very put off by this ending.

Consequently, the film's ultimate ending is considerably less gruesome. A comment on the nonexclusivity of friendship and exploitation, it begins with Virgil mugging an old schoolmate. As they reminisce about the local band, Virgil swipes his friend's watch; as they recall football games, Virgil politely asks for his coat. The robbery doesn't intrude on the nostalgia, nor does nostalgia preclude theft. Isn't the world both "heaven and saints and angels" and "people cashing in"? The twist is that Virgil's friend is also of this mind. After Virgil has relieved him of his last valuable, the friend sorrowfully recalls, "Oh, Virgil, I just remembered I'm a cop" and arrests him. As with Woody, up and down from the barroom floor, at last glimpse Virgil is again in prison and again whittling soap: "Anyone know if it's raining?"

Though this is by far the more suitable ending for *Take the Money and Run,* the first ending is also significant. Its pathos anticipates *Manhattan,* and its attempt to mix broad humor and grim situations will be compellingly recalled in *Love and Death, Stardust Memories,* and *The Floating Lightbulb.*

Bananas

But these works are in the future. *Take the Money and Run* won Allen a loyal, but still small, camp of popular and critical supporters and the clout to demand, from United Artists, the creative freedoms he needed. He did not, however, feel free to tackle more serious subject matter, and his second feature, which begins with a new regime and ends with a wedding, is as classically comic as his first and again more in the playful manner of "The Great Renaldo" than the playful-with-a-purpose manner of "The Moose."

Although it still works best in comic fragments, *Bananas* has a stronger story line than *Take the Money and Run,* and its political gags appear more daring than the first feature's social gags. A parody of political commitment in general and Latin American regimes in particular, *Bananas* was released in 1971, the year Allende came to power in Chile and just after the peak of anti-war activity in this country. As Andrew Sarris noted at the time, "It's one thing to beat up little babies and old women, but quite another to ridicule the poverty of Latin America in these supposedly revolutionary times." Sarris was right, and yet because the political fantasy is not, in the words of the Ku Klux Klan routine, *Allen*'s fantasy, there's no wished-for faith to clash with *Bananas'* political cynicism; and this film is finally no more politically provocative than *Take the Money and Run* is socially provocative. As in his first film, Allen's method is to foil subject with approach: the "hot" political event with the "cool" medium of American television, to parodic ends.

Bananas opens on a strong ironic note. The unflappable presence of "Wide World of Sports" commentator Howard Cosell, flanked by excited spectators, sets up expectations of a sports event. But the setting is the South American "banana" republic of San Marcos, where political coups are as common as war in the Marx Brothers' Fredonia. And the upcoming "event" is yet another "fixed" coup, in which General Vargas (an allusion to the *Getting Even* character) is slated to overthrow the current El Presidente. As Cosell reads the scene, "colorful" and "big moment" events go as planned: the President emerges from his palace, the assassin shoots, the old regime falls slow-motion to the ground—like Clyde in *Bonnie and Clyde.* Cosell bursts through the crowd—"This is American television!"—and finding El Presidente beyond words, moves on to interview Vargas, who enlightenedly vows to shut down the newspapers and wipe out the rebel faction. "Good luck to you, sir," says Cosell.

Bananas has two sometimes overlapping plots, the first of which involves the presidency of San Marcos, which passes from El Presidente to General Vargas and then from Vargas to rebel chief Esposito. When Esposito declares Swedish the national language and decrees a compulsory change of underwear on the half hour, a new leader is sought and found in apolitical American Fielding Mellish. Fielding's (Woody's) fate is *Bananas'* more pressing concern. We meet him in the unlikely role of Execucizer (exercise-while-you-work) demonstrator, disorientedly throwing basketballs and lifting weights while roped into an executive desk. Like Chaplin displaying the factory's eat-while-you-assemble gadget in *Modern Times,* Fielding can't handle work *or* play, much less the two together, and like Woody in "Mechanical Objects," he's pummeled, not liberated, by machines. "I'm not meant for this job," Fielding complains to a fellow demonstrator. Why did he ever leave college? "I was in the black studies program—by now I could have been black."

Though his job remains unsuitable, Fielding's social life brightens when a fashionably liberal young political activist, Nancy (Louise Lasser), solicits his signature for a petition condemning atrocities in San Marcos. Assuring her that he's similarly committed to political causes and Eastern religions, Fielding wonders if Nancy's free for dinner any time in the next six years, and they begin dating. To impress Nancy, Fielding carries placards and gets gassed at rallies. And when she leaves him because "something's missing" in their relationship—he's not enough of a leader for her—Fielding consoles himself with a trip to her favorite cause, San Marcos. There unlikely events conspire to make him first a rebel and then president, in which guise he again courts and now wins Nancy's love. So in the film's last shot, as in its first, Howard Cosell brings us "The Wild World of Sports": this time Nancy and Fielding consummating marriage.

Like "Viva Vargas" before and *Sleeper* after it, *Bananas* is no more indulgent of rebel than of dictator. Esposito and Vargas are equally ridiculous, and Esposito may be more dangerous. For while the general flees to Miami's Fontainbleu Hotel, the "people's" leader turns his palace lawn into a fairground and, in *Bananas*' game execution equivalent to *Duck Soup*'s game war, ties his enemies to wooden stakes for the citizens to shoot at.

As will be true in *Manhattan*, *Bananas*' central incongruity is the fact of a society so morally and intellectually flaccid that Woody (by turns Fielding and Isaac) is its most enlightened citizen. And, as in *Duck Soup* (a major influence here and even more so in *Sleeper*), many of the best political gags are collisions between man the political animal and man the animal. Frequently, *Bananas* alludes to the absurdity of entrusting power to a creature who wants to fill his belly at least three times a day. In a previously observed joke, Fielding, like the

"Viva Vargas" narrator, is asked to feed the rebel troops. Where the narrator picks poisoned mushrooms, Fielding orders "out" from the nearest café: 1,000 grilled cheese, 300 tuna, and 200 bacon-lettuce-and-tomato sandwiches, and coleslaw wheel-barrowed into the hills by white-capped delivery boys. In another eating gag, Fielding is invited to the palace for dinner and turns up with a small white cake box for his host, General Vargas. "He brings cake for a group of people," scoffs the chief-of-state, "he doesn't even bring an assortment."

While San Marcos is *Bananas'* principal setting, Latin American politics is far from its exclusive target, and most of the political gags are no more specifically political than Pat Nixon kissing Henry Kissinger in Allen's PBS special. In one scene a planeload of American soldiers en route to San Marcos wonder whom they're backing: "This time the CIA's not taking any chances," one man explains—half will support the dictator, half the rebels. When Fielding is brought to trial as a suspected spy, J. Edgar Hoover comes to court bearing incriminating telephone tapes of Fielding's heavy breathing, disguised as a black woman, and Miss America tries to testify against Fielding but can get no further than her contest song. The religious jokes are similarly broad: it is the Jewish charity UJA rather than the CIA that supports Vargas, and a cigarette-selling priest takes his cue from Woody's vodka-selling rabbi, absolving buyers, "You stick to New Testament cigarettes, and all is forgiven."

Though its plot is more cogent than *Take the Money and Run's*, *Bananas'* cinematic allusions are similarly varied: *Potemkin's* baby carriage works its way into Esposito's palace coup; *Tom Jones* establishes protocol for Fielding's coffee-slurping, masticating seduction of a San Marcos rebel; and *Modern Times, Duck Soup,* and American television references abound. One of *Bananas'* longest sequences *seems* to be a parody of Robert Altman's 1970 *M*A*S*H* (though, in fact, Allen saw *M*A*S*H* for the first time a few years later, when he was in Paris shooting *Love and Death*). Here Fielding visits his surgeon parents while they operate. Because the Mellishes, Senior, are, like their son, unable to concentrate on two tasks simultaneously, they neglect their bleeding patient to harass their

delinquent son: "Go to college! . . . or who will I leave the
hospital to?" Insisting that surgery isn't so difficult, they hand
Fielding a scalpel and invite him to poke around. Which he
does, giggling and finally noticing, "I think you're losing the
patient." Unaware of his condition, the patient wonders if he'll
be out in time for the theater.

Bananas solves the problem of Chaplin allusions by mixing
and often intermixing them with Hope, Groucho, and gleefully
mean-spirited W.C. Fields homages. A subway "silent film"
mugging sequence is indicative. When a woman in an adjacent
subway seat is brutally assaulted, Fielding at first assumes a
Hope-like pose of cowardly preoccupation (with his *Orgasm*
magazine), but finally tackles the larger, more numerous enemy
as awkwardly and gallantly as would Chaplin. And the influence of Groucho Marx is felt throughout the film: in Fielding's
eccentric courtroom walk and description of his trial as "a
travesty of a mockery of a sham"; in a scene where Fielding,
now president of San Marcos, is greeted in New York by an
official South American translator, who repeats his English in
heavily accented English. The best of the Groucho-like gags are
in the trial scene where Fielding the lawyer shrewdly questions
Fielding the insolent defendant:

> *Fielding:*   I would not joke with this court.
> *Fielding:*   Wouldn't you, or couldn't you?

Though as comically sinned against as Virgil and the upcoming Miles of *Sleeper,* Fielding is the most pugnacious of Allen's
early prototypes. While Virgil and Miles are overwhelmed by
life as it is, Fielding initiates trouble. When a buxom woman
walks his way, he tugs at her breast. When he spots a car being
parallel parked, he helps smash it into the car behind it. Distraught at the unfairness of life and Nancy, Fielding—this time
inadvertently—slams a door shut on his friend's hand; and, as
the friend winces, Fielding throws up his arms in self pity: "See
what I mean?" As will be true, in a more serious context, with
Sandy Bates, we have very mixed feelings about Fielding, which
give way to tentative identification: first, because of the extrem-
ity of his situation and finally because he changes.

For the subtle difference between *Take the Money and Run*

and *Bananas* is that Fielding *does* grow. Like Virgil, he begins as a career and social loser. The receptionist in his office refuses a date because she's showing pornographic movies to friends, not him; and Nancy agrees to see Fielding only when there's no political, yoga, Eastern religion, or feminist event scheduled. Once Nancy knows Fielding better, she decides not to see him at all, proving that he—like Woody in the club routines—can't hold onto a girl.

And yet, in contrast to both Virgil and Woody, by the end of *Bananas* Fielding has taken a qualified first step toward the objective good fortune of the later personae. A first step, because he wins the presidency and, more important, the girl; qualified because his country's chief resources are locusts and hernias, and the circumstances of his intimately related achievements are absurd. The leadership falls to him, not on his own merits, but because everyone else is more egregiously undereducated, self-interested, and craven than he. And Nancy falls in love, not with Fielding, but with Fielding in a removable beard, posing as a leader.

In retrospect, there's something overprotesting about these qualifications, which are smokescreen for the more aggressive, winner qualities Allen is cautiously granting his persona. Though still alienated from conventional society, Fielding, unlike Virgil, is not intimidated by authority figures. He disputes the palace dinner bill with Vargas, talks back to Esposito, and quickly earns the respect of the rebel troops. Where Virgil winds up behind bars, a social and media enigma, Fielding ends up in a Miami wedding bed, a social and media celebrity. He even wins the climactic marriage bout with Nancy. And furthermore, like Allan Felix, Fielding, for all his inadequacies, is unusually discriminating. He has illusions of a perfect mate and, while he'll "pounce" on just about any female, he loves selectively. When Nancy asks if he loves her, Fielding rejoins, "Yes, of course, I love ya." But when required to define love, he circles the issue:

> To love. I love you, I want you in a way of cherishing
> your totality and your otherness, and in the sense of
> a presence and a being and a whole, a coming and
> a going in a room with great fruit . . .

In other words, Fielding, like *Annie Hall*'s Alvy Singer, "lurves" and "loveyas," but is too much the romantic perfectionist to commit himself to one imperfect beloved. Already in *Bananas,* the first film in which he wins an initially reticent woman he wants, the persona is wistfully longing for something better, the magic in the Great Persky's cabinet.

But that wistful longing, born of a discrepancy between love as it is and love as it might be, is not so compelling as it *will* be in Allen's volatile, unpredictable couplings with Diane Keaton. In contrast to the Virgil/Louise romance, Fielding and Nancy's courtship is both believable and distinctive. But their chemistry is comfortable, rather than exciting. Both Allen and Lasser bring quick New York humor and well-matched wits to their scenes together, but erotic and emotional tensions are weak. Their break-up scene, for instance, is played exclusively for laughs, as Fielding suggests and Louise both dismisses and confirms qualities which might be "missing" for her in their relationship. For instance:

> *Fielding:* Is it that I'm not smart enough?
> *Nancy:* No, it's not the fact that you're not smart enough . . .

And it's not the fact that she doesn't love him, though she doesn't.

With the twist that next door is a matter of city blocks, Allen and Lasser's is a girl-next-door love affair, not unlike that of Eddie Bracken and Betty Hutton in Preston Sturges's *Miracle at Morgan's Creek.* As in the Sturges film, the girl is more attractive, more socially acceptable, more obviously the desirable mate, while the boy is more ardent and lovably eccentric. Like Bracken and Hutton, Allen and Lasser are at once an idiosyncratic and a logical pair. Scratch their superficial differences, and there's a fundamental sameness of background and attitude. And the romantic thrust of *Bananas,* as of *Miracle at Morgan's Creek,* is toward a scratching of surfaces to evoke this comforting sameness.

The Allen/Lasser sameness is, of course, not as comforting as most, since shared narcissism and chronic discontent do not bode especially well for a lasting union. As Howard Cosell cheerfully notes in *Bananas'* last scene, "It's hard to tell what will happen in the future. They may live happily ever after. Again, not." And if not, it will only prove what Nancy/Lasser noted early on—that there's "something missing."

Play It Again, Sam

The "something" that is missing between Fielding and Nancy is very much in evidence when Linda Christie bursts through the door of Allan Felix's apartment in the 1972 movie version of *Play It Again, Sam.* For movie audiences, the Allen/Keaton relationship begins here, with Keaton's blonde head bobbing a half head above Allen's and he matter-of-factly finishing off her sentences. In *From Reverence to Rape,* Molly Haskell says of Katherine Hepburn and Spencer Tracy, "While preserving their individuality, they united to form a whole greater than the sum of its parts . . . Out of their complementary incongruities, they created one of the most romantic couples the cinema has ever known." And while their "complementary incongruities" are different, this description applies to Allen and Keaton as well. From *Play It Again, Sam* through *Annie Hall,* Keaton's nature, talents, and movie affinity for, by turns, Allan, Miles, Boris, and Alvy will affect all aspects of Allen's art; while the fact of their fundamental romantic "rightness," unquestioned before *Manhattan,* will be held as litmus paper to test the impact of contemporary society and of life itself on love relationships.

There are two important aspects to Allen's relationship with Keaton. On the one hand, she's "the other," the tall, fair, genteel, conventionally beautiful WASP, while he's small, lower class, "kinda ugly" and, as Annie will note in *Annie Hall,* "a real Jew." Particularly in *Sleeper* and *Annie Hall,* where her intelligence is an issue between them, Keaton's "otherness" has overtones of *Portnoy's Complaint.* "You think I'm stupid," whines Luna to Miles in *Sleeper.* And why should he? She has a college degree in oral sex and is a poetess of greeting-card renown. In *Annie Hall,* Alvy urges adult education courses on Annie (until she develops an interest in one of the professors), who frequently observes that Alvy's first two wives were Jewish intellectuals, but "you don't think I'm smart enough to take seriously." Temperamentally they differ in ways typical of their backgrounds: Keaton is philosophically impressionable and physically dauntless, and Allen is set in his values and afraid of anything he "can't reason with or kiss or fondle."

Yet, obvious differences notwithstanding, Allen and Keaton are uncannily alike. As is established in their opening discussion of aspirin versus Darvon in *Play It Again, Sam,* both are neurotic, insecure, and vividly imaginative. Even more than Allen, Keaton is suggestible, turning from debutante to rebel under the influence of Erno in *Sleeper, becoming* Stanley Kowalski during Miles's deprogramming. And like Allen's, her mind switches between fantasy and reality, to pragmatic as well as hysterical effect. She copes with poverty and a punishing Russian winter in *Love and Death* by devising an ingenious variety of "sleet" dishes and solemnly vows to marry Boris as her mind races:

> Yes, he loves me and would make a devoted hus-
> band, not too exciting, but devoted. We'd have a
> family, maybe not our own, we could rent one
> . . . Me, Boris, and six rented children.

While their opposition heightens erotic and romantic tensions, there's also a sense in which Allen and Keaton are one whole being, redividing throughout, and even within, their films. Sometimes sexual differences are stressed. In the early scenes of *Sleeper,* for instance, Keaton plays a fashionable society female to Allen's ungainly, long-haired hippie male; and in *Play It Again, Sam,* her luminous femininity is juxtaposed to his gawky, lubricious maleness. But there's also a boyish quality to Keaton, who can be more like Woody—e.g., more scheming, verbally agile, and romantically thwarted—than Woody himself. In the beginning of *Love and Death,* for example, when Sonia pragmatically marries and systematically betrays an old herring merchant. Later, when Sonia marries Boris, she fleetingly assumes the role of devoted wife, which she abandons to play a brotherly Bing Crosby to Boris's Hope in their scheme to assassinate Napoleon. And while that scheme hinges on Sonia's sexual ruses, it is as devoid of erotic energy as if Boris himself were seducing the general, and in a sense he is.

Allen's and Keaton's role changes are dizzying, but also seamless. Certain traits are constant—she's always the more socially acceptable, he, the more reliable, partner—but many others are in flux. She is by turns his foil, pal, sex object, and nemesis; Crosby to his Hope, Harpo to his Groucho, Hepburn to his Tracy. He's her Jewish Pygmalion, her conscience, and the above as well. There's a pleasing lack of competition to the love of Allen and Keaton and no fixed rhythm or "schtik" to their palaver. In contrast to Lasser, Keaton can appreciate, without trying to top, Allen's wit, and he gallantly permits her a last laugh now and again, frequently through a physical gesture, as in the shot in *Play It Again, Sam* where Allan swaggers off to "score" with Linda's friend Sharon, and Linda predicts defeat with raised eyebrows.

Differences between the play and the movie version of *Play It Again, Sam*, directed by Herbert Ross, are slight: the setting is now San Francisco, and the new love interest, Barbara, has been deleted from the final scene. Allen says that the play's tight structure forbade new material, so most of the options were directorial. And while contemporary critics missed the wild spontaneity of *Take the Money and Run* and *Bananas*, Ross's tamer approach shows this most conventional of Allen's dramatic vehicles to best advantage.

As does the play, the movie succeeds on the strength of its character relationships. As uncomplicated as they will ever be, Allen and Keaton look immediately right together, with the almost caricaturishly robust Tony Roberts as fitting dramatic and physical foil for them both. Wisely, Ross portrays Allan's fantasy companions Bogart and Nancy as the full characters Allan envisions. Often Bogart is inconveniently real, loudly issuing inappropriate "pouncing" orders and physically intruding on Allan's real-life intimacy with Linda. Thus, Ross stresses the infelicitous aspects of vivid fantasy life, underscoring Allen's message.

Although less outrageous than Allen's own directorial work, *Play It Again, Sam* is filled with off-beat comic images. In one scene, Allan blow-dries his hair and everything else in the room. In another, a happily oblivious variation on distraught Fielding's door-slamming escapade in *Bananas,* Allan is so buoyed by his successful night with Linda that he skips across the Golden Gate Bridge, patting the backs of total strangers. One such stranger is a gentleman seated on the bridge's ledge, engrossed in his newspaper. When Allan taps him, the gentleman falls noiselessly into the bay, newspaper still open in his hands; and the unnoticing perpetrator skips elatedly on.

The deletion of the play's last scene, in which Allan seems about to fall in love with a young film aficionado, is appropriate. As will be true with *Sleeper, Love and Death,* and *Annie Hall* as well, the chemistry between Allen and Keaton is so strong that comparisons are inevitably invidious. (In *Annie Hall* Allen will use invidious comparisons to stress the romantic rightness of Keaton.) The fact that Allan and Linda part is a comment not on their feelings for one another, but on social and moral pressures: love is sacrificed to loyalty, selfishness to honor. Ironies notwithstanding, *Play It Again, Sam*'s resolution acquiesces to the very romantic comedy formula *Annie Hall*'s far more poignant break-up will so profoundly challenge.

Everything You Always Wanted to Know About Sex

After finishing *Play It Again, Sam,* Allen moved directly into production for *Everything You Always Wanted to Know about Sex,* his weakest film, though an important learning experience. Allen recalls, "With my first two films I just wanted to get on the boards. I wanted to be funny, and I couldn't have cared less how they looked. With *Everything You Always Wanted to Know about Sex,* I relaxed a bit and began to think about improving my style."

Allen's style *is* more sophisticated here, though not nearly as distinguished as it will be in *Sleeper;* but dramatic and thematic tensions are weak. A compendium of seven very unequally successful sketches, *Everything You Always Wanted to Know About Sex* gleans its title and parodic target from Dr. Reuben's chatty bestseller of the period. A Reuben question, such as "Are

Transvestites Homosexuals?" introduces each self-contained
segment. Woody stars in four, and all convey the one-note
message that it's absurd, not to mention unerotic, to presume
that one can be *told* everything one wants to know about sex.

As in his first two films, Allen's subject matter precludes an
intellectual conflict: needless to say, Allen is no more compelled
by the "fantasy" that sex manuals work than by social and
political remedies; and, as in the club acts, he's less inclined to
generalize on sex than on political and social issues. While
Allen's later stories and films will contemplate the anarchic
sexual urge in (often infelicitous) relation to love, *Everything
You Always Wanted to Know about Sex* rarely goes deeper than
broad sexual farce. Politics may be the fashionably liberal girl,
but sex is usually enormous breasts and "pouncing." Parts of
the first two sketches and all of the concluding "What Happens
During Ejaculation?" are welcome exceptions.

Set in a medieval castle, the first sketch, "Do Aphrodisiacs
Work?" opens with the disquieting (for Allen) nonsexual absurdity of a court jester sent to jail for not being funny. When
ordered to amuse the king (Anthony Quayle) and his supper
party, the fool (Woody) rattles a miniature version of himself
and strives for Virgil Starkwell's admixture of insolence and
obsequiousness:

> Good evening, your majesty, it's great to be back
> here at the palace. You know what the palace is—
> that's twenty-four living rooms with a dungeon.

When no one cracks a smile, the fool giggles and tries again:

> But seriously, ladies and germs, that plague is really
> something. Doesn't everything look black?

"Not funny," proclaims the king, who sentences the fool—
every comedian in comic extreme—to the dungeon for his troubles.

The king's verdict notwithstanding, Woody's court jester bit
is far more amusing and emotionally real than the sex romp that
follows: a *Midsummer Night's Dream* spoof in which the queen

(Lynn Redgrave) sips a bubbling aphrodisiac and perceives Woody the nebbish as Woody the stud. As with so much of *Everything You Always Wanted to Know about Sex,* the idea of Woody as fool seducing Redgrave as queen is neither erotic nor sufficiently outrageous. After *Play It Again, Sam* and *Bananas,* Woody's conquest comes as no surprise: indeed, the aphrodisiac, like Fielding's winning Nancy as El Presidente, is an over-protesting qualifier. This sketch does have some funny one-liners, however. When the fool's equivalent to Hamlet's father's ghost appears and bids his son to seduce the queen, Woody demurs: "I can't screw above my station." And as the fool fumbles with the queen's obdurate chastity belt, he muses, "I must think of something quickly, because before you know it the Renaissance will be here, and we'll all be painting."

Thanks in good part to Gene Wilder's gentle zaniness, the second sketch, "What is Sodomy?" is more consistently amusing. The outlandish premise here is that a grown, happily married, and moral American doctor could fall so passionately in love with a Greek sheep that he'd swipe her from her current Greek lover, his patient, and sacrifice home and profession to be near her. As with all Allen's best humor, this outlandishness is rooted in truths—or here aphorisms—such as "love is blind" and "physician, heal thyself."

"What is Sodomy?"'s increasingly absurd plot line is carefully observed: beginning with Wilder and his middle-class wife at a conventional breakfast, it builds to Wilder's stolen hotel room moments with sheep lover Daisy and ends with Wilder as a Woolite-guzzling Bowery bum. Interestingly, the thematic concerns of "What is Sodomy?" are, albeit *in extremis,* uncannily like those of *Manhattan.* What happens when a middle-aged man falls in love with a young girl? Can one advise a friend or client on his love life when one is in love with the "woman" in question? A nice visual irony here is that Wilder, with his furry hair and translucent blue eyes, looks a little sheeplike himself. When he lies in bed with the bleating Daisy, there's a physical rightness as well as outrageousness to their mating.

Allen says that the shooting of *Everything You Always Wanted to Know about Sex*'s third sequence, "Why Do Some Women Have Trouble Reaching Orgasm?" was one of his most enjoyable filmmaking experiences. A parody of Antonioni's elaborate tracking and circular shots in films like *La Notte* and *L'Avventura,* Allen's cinematography is agreeably virtuosic, but his story is pedestrian. Woody plays an Italian husband whose macho identity is threatened when his young bride, played by Lasser, gets no joy from their sexual relations. What to do? Woody paces through long narrow corridors and consults with friends, in Italian, but to no avail. Their problem is solved when Lasser discovers the dangerous thrills of sex in public places, and the young couple begin "window shopping" in fashionable boutiques. The idea has possibilities, but plot and character developments are strictly parodic and unsurprising.

Want of a comic twist or emotional depth characterizes the following three sketches as well. In "Are Transvestities Homosexuals?" a middle-aged husband and father gets the urge to "come out of the closet" while dining with the parents of his daughter's fiancé. Played by Lou Jacobi, this long-repressed transvestite runs through the quiet suburban streets in high-heeled shoes and his hostess's tailored gown. Where the Italian skit is insufficiently outrageous, this sketch is merely silly. Its one amusing moment is the anguished wife's complaint: "I love you. You love me. You could have come to me and said, 'Tess, I have a diseased mind, I'm a sick individual. I need help, I need treatment, I'm perverted . . .' "

In the following episode, "What Are Sex Perverts?" a sexually perverse variation on Woody's vodka-selling rabbi is made "pervert of the week" on the guess-the-"fascinating-fetish" television game show. This rabbi's fetish, fulfilled on the show, is to watch his wife eat pork while a scantily clad young woman whips him and murmurs, "Naughty rabbi." Some critics complained of anti-Semitism but, as with the smoker-absolving Catholic priest in *Bananas,* this gag is basically nonsectarian and also, in the words of Anthony Quayle's king, "not funny."

The opening of "Are the Findings of Doctors and Clinics Who Do Sexual Research Accurate?" shows a bit more promise. Woody and a young sex reporter, Helen (Heather Macrae), pay a visit to the secluded Gothic sex research center of a famed Dr. Bernardo (John Carradine). Greeted *Frankenstein*-style by Bernardo's lackey, they soon find they've been slated as sexual guinea pigs in the mad Bernardo's current experiment. Some amusing *Frankenstein*-genre parodies ensue but too soon give way to a frantic search for the escaped breast—a man-made gland which smothers its victims to death. After the breast suffocates a lover's lane couple, Woody manages to ensnare it in a giant bra, and all is sexually well. Again, there's humor to this concept, but its working out is curiously listless.

The final "What Happens During Ejaculation?" sketch, on the other hand, is at once ebulliently outrageous and underlyingly serious. Answering Dr. Reuben in his own spacecraft imagery, its opening shot is a facsimile of Stanley Kubrick's launching pad in *2001*. This launching pad represents the body organism whose "object" is intercourse and whose "missile" is a penis peopled by white-cloaked sperm (Woody timidly among them). For the mission to succeed, a fettucini dinner, a bad conscience, and the intimidating thought that the "space" desired belongs to a college graduate must be overcome.

While most of the earlier sketches stress the obvious absurdity of a purely mental approach to the physical act of sex, "What Happens During Ejaculation?" is more intelligently satirical. By introducing a mental "control room operator," a conscience, and a timid sperm as material presences, Allen underscores the real, often troublesome function of the mind in all sexual endeavors. What is absurd about the Dr. Reuben self-help approach to sex, this sketch intimates, is not that it dismisses the role of the body, but that it presumes that the mind can be "taught" the appropriate sexual yen.

"What Happens During Ejaculation?" moves swiftly and assuredly from start to successful "Take off!" As control room operators, Tony Randall and Burt Reynolds are as authoritative and jovial as Dr. Reuben himself. "Think we're gonna have intercourse tonight?" Randall asks his staff. "I'm hopeful, very hopeful," responds a nerve ending. Meanwhile, the stomach absorbs a fettucini dinner, the eye gazes across the restaurant table at a pretty college graduate, and one sperm, Woody, experiences travel anxieties. ("You took an oath when you entered sperm-training school to fertilize an ovum or die trying," he is warned.) A black sperm wonders how he got here.

While continuing to make perfect emotional sense, Allen's

spaceship parable grows increasingly ludicrous. "We're gonna try and ball her right here in the car," announces Reynolds, who then orders, "Roll out the tongue." With his next announcement, "Here come the tits!" the whole launching pad trembles, and the mission is delayed because a priest is discovered "sabotaging the expedition by playing around with guilt." But the priest is soon evicted, and as the entire erection staff chants, "My eyes have seen the glory . . ." and the brain cells call out baseball players' names, Woody is successfully thrust into inner space. In the sketch's last shot, Mission Control is celebrating with champagne and speculating about a repeat performance.

As this final sketch vividly demonstrates, the trouble with most of *Everything You Always Wanted to Know about Sex* is not its subject, but Allen's lightly parodic approach. The sexual issues he glances over here will be provocatively considered later, just as social issues alluded to in *Take the Money and Run* will be seriously contemplated in *Sleeper* and *Manhattan.* The virtues of Allen's first three directorial efforts, and of the movie version of *Play It Again, Sam,* are considerable. Here Allen translates his nightclub and playwriting gifts into the film medium, explores visual surrealism, and introduces the film persona as a more romantically and socially promising creature than the fellow who got attacked by his doorman in the early club routine. Most important, Allen here gleans the knowledge and confidence to move into his major work, which begins with his next two films.

=5=

Turning Point

Sleeper,   Love and Death

Sleeper marks the turning point between Allen as a film comic and Allen as a comic film artist. In visual continuity and complexity, the difference between *Bananas* and *Sleeper* parallels Allen's verbal development between the early and the late nightclub monologues. As previously discussed, the style of *Take the Money and Run, Bananas,* and, to a lesser extent, *Everything You Always Wanted to Know about Sex* is a loose mixture of parody and self-parody. And while Allen quickly tired of this sort of thing, he found his options somewhat limited. "I'm sometimes forced to make shots that are more simple and less imaginative because I don't want the imagination of the shot to intrude on the laugh . . . simplicity is paramount to comedy, and simplicity is not always the best kind of shot," Allen told Lax in the early seventies.

By juxtaposing Antonioni's eloquent cinematography with Woody's prosaic person, Allen addresses this dilemma parodically in the Italian segment of *Everything You Always Wanted to Know about Sex,* and in *Sleeper* he makes the eloquent style his own. The key to maintaining the broad joke while enriching the cinematogrphy was to stress an incongruity. The joke in the visually imaginative opening shots of *Sleeper* is: what is sloppy, ethnic, maladroit Woody doing in this silent comedy futureworld run by machines? Or, in the beginning of *Love and Death,* why is the raspy New York voice of Woody commingling with stately Prokofiev music as clouds swirl over nineteenth-century Russia?

Consciously or subliminally, the look of *Sleeper* and *Love and Death* derives from Leo McCarey, who directed such Marx Brothers films as *Duck Soup,* and from animator/filmmaker Frank Tashlin, who directed Bob Hope in *Son of Paleface.* In his cuts back and forth between the distinct realms of reality and fantasy, Allen's aesthetic and philosophical connections to McCarey are the more obvious. Their comments on war, in *Duck Soup* and *Love and Death* respectively, are indicative. When Fredonia goes to war in *Duck Soup,* McCarey cuts from Harpo twirling a cheerleader's baton to a fantasy sports event montage (swimming meets, crew races, etc.) and then back to Harpo in Fredonia. When Russia declares war in *Love and Death,* Allen similarly cuts from a reaction shot of the dumbfounded Woody/Boris, to a fantasy sports stadium montage (cheerleaders, a "blini man" selling Russian fast food in the bleachers), and then back to Boris in Russia. In each case the sports montage, at once character's fantasy and author's interjection, is unambiguously derisive: war is an elevation of man's competitive instincts and no more imperative than an athletic event. But also in each case, the arrangement of images complicates the polemics. For while Herbert Ross conveys Allan's similarly full-bodied real and fantasy acquaintances within the same frame in *Play It Again, Sam,* stressing a seamless connection, McCarey and Allen here differentiate the two worlds, subtly noting that concept must contend with actuality. While Harpo and Woody may *perceive* war as no more urgent than sports, this game threatens their lives.

Sometime-cartoonist Frank Tashlin's influence on Allen is subtler, but equally important. In contrast to both Ross and McCarey, Tashlin juxtaposes real with animated-seeming characters within the same film frame. His use of Bob Hope in the unconventional western *Son of Paleface* is a good example. Here Hope, playing an Eastern greenhorn, is realistically portrayed, while Tashlin's camera makes most of the native cowboys and girls look like cut-outs pasted against a western backdrop. The effect is a curious one. For, on the one hand, he's conspicuously out of his element. And, similarly, within the surreal worlds of *Sleeper* and *Love and Death,* the two-dimensional look of Erno the handsome rebel and Ivan the "Neanderthal" brother simultaneously underscores and diminishes the alienation of more *visually* substantial Miles and Boris. In a cinematic affirmation of *Bananas'* theme, it's a curious world indeed when a small, bespectacled, "kinda ugly" man is the most normal-looking character on the screen.

While there's no dearth of stylistic allusions in either *Sleeper* or *Love and Death,* the connections are now fluid, and Allen the artist pointedly disassociates himself from Miles and Boris the personae. This discrepancy is playfully suggested in *Sleeper* when Allen's camera watches impassively as Miles gets hopelessly embroiled in celluloid knots, and more jarringly in *Love and Death* when Allen cuts away from his dying persona to observe the bored Sonia at home. Although Allen is yet to discover the thematic correlative for his fragmented genre plots, the chemistry between Allen and Keaton deepens *Sleeper*'s and *Love and Death*'s now only superficially outrageous love stories.

Sleeper

Set two hundred years in the future in a country known as Central Parallel of the United States, *Sleeper* opens as two Underground scientists eagerly await the "second coming" of cryogenically preserved Miles Monroe. Formerly a "Greenwitch Village" health food entrepreneur and clarinet player, this artifact of the 1970s will, they hope, help change the banal state of affairs in Central Parallel today. As Dixieland jazz plays gaily on the soundtrack, Miles/Woody glides into the scene in a white capsule (reminiscent of the cake box Fielding offers Vargas in *Bananas*), is unfurled from an aluminum foil carapace like a Stouffer's dinner, and stumbles back to life, looking like a cross between Harold Lloyd and Chaplin during the nervous breakdown scene in *Modern Times.* After his two-hundred-year nap, Miles is gently lowered into a wheel chair and handed a glutinous blue baby food, which he smears all over the pristine scene of his birth: a very sane, very Woody-like response, indeed.

With old movies and contemporary social mores as subtext allusions, *Sleeper*'s plot is a mixture of road movie romance and cat-and-mouse chase between Miles, christened "the alien," and the Central Parallel powers that be. Once recovered from his two-century time lapse, Miles is briefed on the crisis of superficiality in modern life. Led by a telescreen personality, served by robots, and enlightened by Rod McKuen, this society is, Miles readily concedes, "even worse than California." By systematically "reprogramming" eccentricities, the government keeps most everyone mechanically happy. Still, there's an Underground who urge Miles, as the state's only unregistered citizen, to infiltrate the government's secret Aries Project and overthrow the technocratic regime. Although his political activities have hitherto been limited ("for twenty-four hours once I refused to eat grapes"), the threat of "reprogramming" whets Miles's social indignation. Disguised as a domestic robot, he enters the Establishment household of greeting card poetess Luna, who, at first against her will and finally with enthusiasm, helps him replace one bad government with another.

Where *Take the Money and Run* and *Bananas* parody randomly, *Sleeper* concentrates on early film comedies. Laurel and Hardy's pie-throwing debacles are recalled in the opening scene where "reborn" Miles smacks everyone he confronts with a paper plate of blue baby food. Groucho's and Harpo's famous mirror routine is affectionately spoofed in a shaving sequence where Miles discovers strangers, rather than his own soapy face, staring at him from the looking glass. And the factory episodes in *Modern Times* are ingeniously evoked as *Sleeper*'s robots twirl around on a carousel, waiting for their heads to be unscrewed. The most Buster Keatonesque of Allen's films, *Sleeper*'s visual gags often transform Miles into some sort of moving vehicle. As he flees the police, wildly flapping his arms above a defective Japanese flying belt, Miles looks like an airplane struggling to take flight. When an assailant's bullet punctures his "alien" suit, he and Luna course through the water like a speedboat.

As well as co-writing, directing, and starring, Allen plays

clarinet in the Dixieland scores which insouciantly counter-point *Sleeper*'s visual surrealism. And, in their first script collaboration, Marshall Brickman's facility for sophisticated social satire is also keenly felt. Where *Take the Money and Run* focuses on mass social discontent and maladjustment, *Sleeper* observes the absurd social pleasures of a privileged few. The subtle difference between these two satirical visions is a matter of propinquity rather than depth: while Allen and Brickman are no more compelled by the "fantasy" of social bromides than by that of social solutions, the former are more annoyingly with them.

The satire in *Sleeper*'s early scenes, before Miles meets Luna, is mostly broad comic attacks on social fads, faiths, and celebrities. Presented with a bland meal, Miles comments, "This stuff tastes awful. I could have made a fortune selling it in my health food restaurant." And his confidence in modern medicine is shaken when he remembers entering the hospital in 1973: "My doctor said I'd be on my feet in five days. He was off by 199 years." Society as Miles knew it came to an end, he is informed, when Albert Shanker (the volatile head of New York City's teachers' union) "got hold of a nuclear warhead." But certain vestiges of pre-World War III life remain. At the scientists' request, Miles identifies a slide of Charles de Gaulle: "a very famous French chef, had his own television show." Norman Mailer is "a very great writer. He donated his ego to the Harvard Medical School." As they watch a tape of Nixon's Checkers Speech, one scientist muses, "Some of us have a theory that he might have been a President of the United States, but that he did something so horrendous that all records, everything was wiped out about him." (As Maurice Yacowar points out in *Loser Take All,* this gag predates Watergate.)

Man's slothful dependence on machines is parodied through *Sleeper*'s working class: robots, who in a single breath can unperturbedly announce, "The security police are here, and are surrounding the house," and wonder, "When will you be wanting lunch?" And *Sleeper* gets underway as the Underground scientists are carried off for "reprogramming," and Miles, posing as a bespectacled domestic robot, is deposited at Luna's door. "Ah, no!" she groans. "Is this the best they could do? I'd hoped for something with at least decent features."

Where Lasser's Woody-like foibles merely reinforce the social and political absurdities in *Bananas,* Keaton's less predictable, increasingly pronounced idiosyncrasies complicate *Sleeper*'s satire. Philosophically, she's as wrong-headed as she is capricious. At the start of the film, her Establishment way of life is absurd, albeitly familiarly: for pleasurable sex she hops in a cylindrical elevator called the Orgasmatron; for relaxation, she rubs a silver Orb ball; for nourishment, she eats only the current health food elixirs—fats, cream pies, hot fudge. Like most Central Parallel citizens, Luna can't understand social discontent:

> This world is so full of wonderful things. What makes people suddenly go berserk and and hate everything? . . . After all, there's the Orb and there's the telescreen and there's the Orgasmatron. What else do they want?

By the middle of the film, she's just as absurdly a Marxist.

Luna's struggle to hold her fickle, inarticulate, pretty female own against Miles's scruffy, verbal, implacably skeptical maleness gives *Sleeper* the romantic edge *Bananas* lacks. The film is best when Allen and Keaton are most nimbly at odds: in an early scene when Luna brings Miles, still her domestic robot, to have his head switched for "something a little more aesthetic," and regally turns her back as he pathetically awaits decapitation. Or when Miles escapes from the head-switching factory and importunes his arrogant but physically fragile employer, "You wouldn't give me away, would you? You're a nice person." At which point she shrieks for help, and in the following shot, he's gagged her.

Significantly, it's the fanatically committed Erno, rather than moral but intelligently conflicted Miles, who captures Luna's romantic imagination and sets her passionately on the rebel's course. Luna is no more converted to Miles's high-minded principles and cynical vision of reality than he is influenced by her intuition of "someone out there who watches over us." Though she pragmatically adapts a friendly attitude, Luna leaps at her first opportunity to betray Miles. And when she reluctantly agrees to help him find the Aries Project and the

Underground, it's only because she too is now pursued for "alien" contamination.

In good romantic comedy tradition, Miles's attraction to the headache-prone, temperamental ("I want to go home!") Luna is subtly intimated from the start. As they flee from the police, through deserted fields, caves, and houses, it's her affection for this smart, unchivalrous (he insists she help him push a car over a cliff) "alien" which, always mistrustfully, grows. As will be ritual with the later persona's women, Luna first appreciates Miles's humor, then finds him oddly attractive, then wants to hop in the Orgasmatron with him:

> *Luna:* Do you want to perform sex with me?

Unlike Virgil and Fielding, Miles "pounces" discriminately and is holding out for something a bit more personal. Soon Luna's whining "You think I'm stupid," to which he truthfully retorts, "I think that you're bright and sensitive and beautiful." He also suspects she's dim-witted, and when the police bear down on him, Miles reminds his fleeing mate where she's headed:

> *Miles:* The Aries Project—can you remember that
> name?
> *Luna:* Yes. The Jupiter Project.

Left on her own, Luna has no trouble finding the Underground and a new rebel boyfriend, Erno.

When Miles is captured and "reprogrammed" by the government, *Sleeper* returns to the broad satire of its early scenes. A few wonderfully outrageous sketches portray the impressionable Miles as an exemplary Establishment citizen. In one, this "kinda ugly" robot tearfully accepts the title of Miss America. In another, he visits the official government tailors, who happen to have sewing machines (with pronounced Jewish noses) as faces and Myron Cohen voices. "You want trousers?" they ask. "We got trousers." Since Miles's attitudes are now programmedly Establishment, Underground Luna is again his philosophical opposite. When she comes to rescue him, Miles orders his robot watch dog to attack. A variation on the ant

Woody's parents give him in the club routine, this dog responds by intoning, "Hello, I'm Rags, woof, woof, woof, woof . . ." And Miles becomes a candidate for re-reprogramming, a superb Method acting spoof in which Luna and Erno recreate the ambience of a Sunday dinner in Brooklyn. When this fails to revive Miles's alien spirit, Luna performs a Marlon Brando speech from *A Streetcar Named Desire*.

Like *Bananas, Sleeper* builds to a madcap political climax which tapers into a romantic comedy denouement. With little help from rebel chief Erno who, in Miles's envious opinion, is off "taking handsome lessons," Miles and Luna ferret out the Aries Project and learn that the nose, all that remains of Central Parallel's leader, is scheduled for cloning. Posing as cloning specialists (Miles: "We're doctors, not imposters"), Miles and Luna work their way into the operating room where, in fine Marx Brothers style, they exhibit both professional and verbal befuddlement:

> *Luna:*   I believe this is going to be a very difficult croning job.
> *Miles:*   Cloning, you idiot, not croning.

Nonetheless, they manage to abduct and overthrow the nose, place Erno in power, and change little in the real world. As Miles patiently explains, "Don't you understand, in six months we'll be stealing Erno's nose? Political solutions don't work."

And yet, in the process of doing their moral best, Miles and Luna have been somewhat compensated. Luna says she loves Miles, who replies, "I don't blame you, honey." And though he believes only in sex and death, and she has learned that love fades—"that was proven by science"—in a more compelling variation on *Bananas,* they may live happily ever after in futureworld.

Whereas Virgil wins Louise posing as a cellist and Fielding courts Nancy as El Presidente, Luna has no illusions about Miles's status or convictions. "You don't believe in science, and you also don't believe that political solutions work, and you don't believe in God," she complains, and he readily agrees. Furthermore, he refuses to ingratiate himself. Though never wantonly or mean-spiritedly aggressive (as was Fielding), Miles gags, bullies, and teases Luna. Yet, Luna chooses Miles over the conventionally handsome and committed Erno for the not so irrational reason that she loves him.

No longer hiding behind false appearances, the persona is not only a lovable, but a demanding character, who wakes up angry. Informed that his "rebirth" is a miracle, he counters: "To me, a miracle of science is I go into the hospital for a minor operation, I come out the next day, and my rent isn't 2,000 months overdue . . . This is what I call a cosmic screwing!" During the course of the film, he wins the girl, overthrows the government, and has the presumption to remain dissatisfied. *Sleeper* throws a new light on the seeming shortcomings of the earlier personae as well. Want of a college education is nothing for Fielding to be ashamed of when Luna can get a degree, majoring in "cosmetics, sexual technique, and poetry." And when beauty goes hand in hand with vacuity, and sexual success leads only to mechanical satisfaction, perhaps it's better to be scruffy, jolted, overeager—and human.

Just as Miles's objective success and subjective discontent anticipate Alvy Singer's, the social trappings of *Sleeper* antici- pate *Annie Hall*. With its Orb for an easy high, its nose for a leader, Luna's banal poetry acclaimed as art, and relaxed Erno as love alternative to anxious Miles, *Sleeper* is often an abstract version of this later film. Yet its differences are also relevant. Using Raymand Durgnat's excellent definition of comedy, *Sleeper*'s outrageous context "disconnects" us from its charac- ters, "enabl[ing] us to share their unpleasant feelings pleasura- bly." We laugh at the end of *Sleeper* when Luna whines, "But Miles, don't you see meaningful relationships between men and women don't last . . . there's a chemical in our bodies that makes it so we all get on each others' nerves sooner or later," not because what she says is preposterous, but because an obser- vation potentially applicable to all has been "pleasurably" dis- tanced from us.

And, as with so many of *Sleeper*'s romantic and social obser- vations, it is Allen's image rather than his insight which is compelling. *Sleeper* never challenges its audience intellectually; rather, with considerable help from David Walsh's crisp cinematography and Dale Hennessy's imaginative set designs,

Allen here paints an inspiredly foolish picture of sophisticated modern life. And in the process he "gets even" with the big egos and petty distractions which trivialize contemporary existence.

Love and Death

Though its tone, look, and outrageous context render *Love and Death* very much the sister work to *Sleeper,* this 1975 film evolves out of different and more complicated ambitions. After *Sleeper* was released and well received at Christmas 1973, Allen started work on a murder mystery script for a June production deadline. Again, a romance between himself and Keaton would be rooted to a classic genre situation, but now the setting was contemporary New York, and Allen told Lax at the time:

> I wanted to do a more human film—comedy but real
> person. Not a guy wakes up in the future, or a guy
> robs a bank, or a guy takes over a Latin American
> country. I wanted to do one where I play me, Diane
> plays her, we live in New York. Conflict but real, as
> opposed to too flamboyant an idea . . .

But June arrived, and still dissatisfied with the murder mystery script (scenes from which will be used in *Annie Hall*), Allen turned to another project, which he then described to Lax as "funny in the sense that one reads an S.J. Perelman essay. It's just crazy, maniacally funny." And *Love and Death is* maniacally funny but, as Allen told me recently, it also reflects the more "real" situations and relationships tackled in the murder mystery script. Allen is still troubled by what he perceives as an "imbalance between the ideas and the crazy comedy" approach of *Love and Death:* "People don't connect with the seriousness of that picture because of the tone." But he's pleased with some of the film's observations, especially on death:

> When Keaton's husband dies, and she says, "Life is
> really terrible—so where do you want to eat?" To
> me that said more about death and how we deal with
> it than I could have if I were being genuinely serious.

Along with romantic love and daydream, *Love and Death* is the first of Allen's films to contemplate the "magic" of art and philosophy. And while Allen may satirize the sublime as ebulliently as he satirizes social mores and pretenses, his yearning toward great art and ideas—skeptical though he may be a) that they exist and b) that he deserves to know them, is as powerful in the artist as it is endearing in the persona. Albert Shanker and health food are topical buzz words in *Sleeper;* Freud and Cosima Wagner are intellectual buzz words in "The Metterling Lists"; Tolstoy, Dostoyevsky, and Ingmar Bergman are at once *Love and Death*'s buzz words—its big thinkers with short laundry lists—and figures Allen finds deeply attractive. The important difference between the thrusts of *Take the Money and Run, Bananas, Everything You Always Wanted to Know about Sex,* and *Sleeper* and of *Love and Death* is that the sacred cow Allen attacks is finally his own.

Like *War and Peace* and *Duck Soup, Love and Death* takes place in a state perpetually on the brink of war; and, like *The Seventh Seal* and *Monsieur Beaucaire,* it continually notes the incompatibility of personal valor and staying alive. *Love and Death* opens in the concept/reality collision spirit of *Getting Even,* with Prokofiev's *Alexander Nevsky* score accompanying Boris's musing:

> How I got into this predicament I'll never know.
> Absolutely incredible. To be executed for a crime I
> never committed. Of course, isn't all mankind ex-
> ecuted for a crime it never committed? The differ-
> ence is all men go eventually, but I go at six o'clock
> tomorrow morning. I was supposed to go at five
> o'clock, but I have a smart lawyer . . .

As clouds whoosh over nineteenth-century Russia, Allen the lofty thinker holds his own against Allen the cunning survivor. And so throughout *Love and Death*, which, like *Take the Money and Run*, seeks a "key" to its protagonist's singularity in his past.

Boris's family is a meeting of Brooklyn and Tolstoy: a guffawing Uncle Nikolai, grandparents who perpetually glower, a father who hugs a clump of dried earth under his coat because "someday I hope to build on it." Always obsessed with death, epistemology, the paradox that some Jews have horns and others stripes, and that Old Gregor should be younger than Young Gregor, the child Boris is alienated from most people and keenly attracted to Cousin Sonia. Sonia, "In addition to being the most beautiful woman I'd ever seen," Boris recalls, "was one of the few people I could have deep conversations with." When the film begins, a mature Boris is still in love with Sonia, who likes him but loves his brother Ivan, who likes her but soon announces his engagement to another woman; at which point Sonia agrees to marry an old herring merchant for spite.

When Napoleon's invasion turns most Russian minds from love to war, Boris remains philosophical: "What good is war? We kill a few Frenchmen, they kill a few Russians, next thing you know it's Easter." Want of enthusiasm notwithstanding, Boris goes off to war and becomes a well-known coward, while Sonia stays home, marries, and earns a reputation for promiscuity.

First the herring merchant dies, then Ivan dies, then Boris is decorated for an inadvertent act of bravery and sent home. When he seduces a voluptuous countess, her count fiancé challenges Boris to a duel. And assuring Sonia that he hasn't a chance to survive, Boris convinces her to marry him should he survive. Boris survives, they marry, Sonia learns to love Boris, who experiences the "happiest time of my life," followed by an urge to commit suicide, which he also survives.

When war returns to Russia, Sonia quotes Attila the Hun that "violence is justified in the service of mankind" and insists they must assassinate Napoleon. Initially arguing for "active fleeing," Boris finally joins Sonia on a *Sleeper*-like chase. Posing as royal Spanish sister and brother, Sonia woos a Napoleon "poseur" to their bedchamber where Boris debates the moral pros and cons of assassinating the bloody dictator. Still undecided, Boris is arrested by the French and visited by God, who promises to spare him the firing squad. But God, it seems, is also a poseur, and as Sonia flees back to the never-changing Russian summerhouse, her husband gets to experience his morbid obsession first-hand.

Love and Death is replete with mind/body, concept/execution, art/life conflicts that, at their most playful, recall the social and political gags in the earlier films. As previously noted, the portentousness of war is deflated in analogous shots of bloodshed and of cheerleaders. And political solutions are again exuberantly undercut in eating gags. When Boris wonders what one wins when one wins a war, his general exclaims, "Imagine your loved ones conquered by Napoleon and forced to live under French rule. Do you want them to eat that rich food and those heavy sauces?" Later Napoleon exhorts his chefs, "We must develop the Napoleon before he develops Beef Wellington. The future of Europe hangs in the balance!"

Many of the broader parodies confront *Love and Death*'s nineteenth-century subject with its author's twentieth-century experience. Anachronisms abound: Sonia's first husband takes his "pet" (a herring) to bed; Boris's army superior is a black American corporal; Boris composes T.S. Eliot's "I should have been a pair of ragged claws . . ." and dismisses it as "sentimental." Connections between Jewish Allen and Russian Orthodox Boris are intimated when the latter is accused of having a yellow streak down his back. Knowing that Jews have stripes, Boris retorts, "It's not down, it's across." And there are numerous conflicts between posture and passion. Boris, for instance, launches into an exegesis on God and otherness as prelude to asking Sonia, "Hey, you dating any Russians I should know about?"

The mind/body conflict in love and death is observed as Sonia searches for a man who "embodies the three great aspects of love—intellectual, spiritual, and sensual"—but loves hulky, mindless Ivan. Or as Sonia responds to her first husband's physical passing by concentrating on her own physical well-being: moments after the herring merchant dies, she's ticking off restaurant options. And Boris too conceives of the afterlife in culinary terms: death, he tells Sonia, "is even worse than the food at Kresge's."

Among the best of *Love and Death*'s collisions are those which note the irrelevance of art to life. Before sending his men off on furlough, Boris's commanding officer stages a cautionary skit which, in no uncertain terms, spells out the medical hazards of promiscuity. When the "little hygiene play" is over, the soldiers applaud, and an enthusiastic spectator announces that he plans to spend the next three days in a brothel. When Boris's father visits him in prison, these two Russians maraud through Dostoyevsky's "oeuvre" in a few desultory sentences:

> *Boris:* He must have been possessed.
> *Father:* Well, he was a raw youth.
> *Boris:* Raw youth! He was an idiot . . . I hear he was a gambler.
> *Father:* You know he could be your double.

And yet the great delight of *Love and Death* is that, for each of these purely playful gags, there's an equally funny but more resonant correlative. There's the war sequence, for instance, in which Boris ruminates, "Wow, the battle looks completely different when you're in the middle of it than it does to the generals on the hill." On its surface, this speech is, of course, a parody of Prince Andrey's battle thoughts in *War and Peace:* the implication being that Tolstoy is as ignorant of what it feels like to be Andrey as Boris, a foot soldier, is ignorant of what it feels like to be a general on the hill.

But the joke pushes further because *War and Peace* is not a "little hygiene play" or a *Sleeper* Orb or a *Bananas* political coup, but a major work of art. Tolstoy's eternal truths will do little for Boris on the battlefield and much for reality-weary Allen, and ourselves, in our studies. If great art neither derives directly from nor assists experience, it is still a profound imaginative release. There's a double contradiction to this *War and Peace* spoof. If Tolstoy is absurd, then we are absurd for appreciating him. And to take this a Sonia-esque step further, as Allen does, is it not absurd that we can appreciate the absurdity of appreciating Tolstoy and still appreciate Tolstoy?

So while surrendering none of its superficial cleverness, this gag deepens with reflection, as do Allen's even more complex observations on death. During the early scenes of *Love and Death,* characters are as foolishly sentimental about their own mortality as they are indifferent to others'. When the herring merchant lies dying, he sees himself "swimming out with the open sea like the great white herring." At this point in the film,

Allen's message seems wryly straightforward: as with Nat Ackerman in "Death Knocks," a little man perceives great events in his own limited vocabulary. Yet later, when Boris himself dies, this earlier scene comes back to haunt us. Admiring herrings, the herring merchant envisions a herring merchant death; admiring Bob Hope and Ingmar Bergman, Allen imagines Boris's/his own dead self dancing a Bob Hope-like turn through a *Seventh Seal* landscape. Thus, the most and least imaginative are similarly condemned to view otherness in concrete, personal terms.

Like the earlier works, *Love and Death* pays a number of parodic homages to favorite films: to *Duck Soup* in the war montage, to *The Seventh Seal* in the death scenes. Eisenstein's triumphal lion montage in *October* is reversed in Boris's slumbrous, post-coital fantasy; and Sonia bids adieu to the dead Boris in the split-face style of Bergman's *Persona*. Like the subway sequence in *Bananas,* Boris's duel with the count evokes both Chaplin and Bob Hope. Like Chaplin in *City Lights*'s boxing match, Boris deftly eludes his far superior opponent by cringing in his shadow; but like Hope in *Monsieur Beaucaire,* he compensates for physical rebuke with absurd verbal truculence. Thus, with bullet wounds in both arms, Boris impishly criticizes the count's singing: "He's got a great voice, doesn't he? I should have killed him."

Yet, more than in the earlier films, Allen here invents his own verbal and visual routines: a twin fantasy sequence in which Sonia frantically contemplates the implications of marriage to Boris while Boris murmurs, "Wheat, wheat . . ."; a vividly drawn "Idiot's Convention" at which Boris and Sonia deposit their Village Idiot, the only happy person they know. Played at double speed, the early marital crises and reconciliations are, like Luna's romantic observations in *Sleeper,* pedestrian truths swiftly and imaginatively observed. And Allen's many juxtapositions of real but cartoon-seeming battle scenes with the unwieldy lifelike Boris are very effective.

Where Miles is a logical extension of Fielding, Boris is a refreshingly thoughtful persona. Though cowardly by nineteenth-century standards, his conscientious objections to war ("You think there's any difference whether we live under the

czar or Napoleon? They're both crooks—the czar's a little
taller.") are astute by our own. And his willingness to risk death
rather than shoot at his duel opponent (the count) is positively
courageous. Where the more plebeian earlier personae were
always compelled to react, Boris has the leisure to contemplate
and, even at the happiest time in his life, find "something missing . . . a void at the center of my being . . ." So Nancy's
practical misgivings about Fielding in *Bananas* have been supplanted by Boris's metaphysical misgivings about life itself.

As with *Sleeper,* the early scenes of *Love and Death* place
Allen and Keaton in conflict. Frequently Keaton's lovely
thought is deflated in Allen's sniggering retort; such as:

> *Sonia:*   Ah, yes, yes, I definitely think this is the
>   best of all possible worlds.
> *Boris:*   It's certainly the most expensive.

And sexual tensions are heightened through their romantic
crossed purposes. But in contrast to Luna and Miles (and in
anticipation of Mary and Isaac in *Manhattan*), Sonia and Boris
are social and intellectual equals. And her instincts are his with
a feminine cast: when he goes uncommittedly off to war, she
goes irreverently into marriage; and she seduces while Boris
assaults first the Spanish nobles they will impersonate, and then
the false Napoleon. The strong imaginative connections between Sonia and Boris are explored in dialogues as seamless as
the fantasy/reality segues in "The Great Renaldo." No matter
how obscure the image Allen conceives, Keaton will sustain it,
and vice versa. Indicative is their discussion of children:

> *Sonia:*   I want children with you.
> *Boris:*   What kind?
> *Sonia:*   Little children.
> *Boris:*   Of course, the big ones are mentally slower.

Love and Death marks two significant developments for
Allen. First, as he had originally intended with *Take the Money
and Run,* the persona dies; now justifiably, for *Love and Death*'s
often underlyingly painful death-related humor prepares for

this eventuality. And yet it is shocking: as Allen cuts from
Boris, complacently seated before a French firing squad, we—
and Boris himself—anticipate a miraculous escape. Like Jimmy
Bond in *Casino Royale,* Boris will have a grenade up his sleeve,
or he will improbably overthrow mortality just as Fielding and
Miles overthrew bad political regimes. Instead, Allen breaks a
fundamental rule of comedy and kills his persona. And while
this death is comically illustrated—with Boris waving and call-
ing heresies (the worst you can say about God is that he's "an
under-achiever") to Sonia, the fact of it is an important narrative and thematic step toward seriousness. The message of *Love
and Death* is: politics is foolish, life is not. While he can ignore
the passing of governments, the most skeptical mortal must
contend with, and finally lose out to, a great mystery.

More interesting still is the new moral dimension *Love and
Death* brings to Allen's work. Where *Bananas* and *Sleeper*
suggest physically precarious dilemmas (whether or not to
overthrow Vargas and the nose, respectively), the ethically
right choice is obvious; as it is when Boris is asked to shoot the
count. But this is not so neatly the case when Boris weighs the
pros and cons of murdering Napoleon:

> If I don't kill him he'll make war all through
> Europe. But murder . . . What would Socrates say?
> All those Greeks were homosexuals. Wow, they
> must have had some wild parties. I bet they took
> houses together on Crete for the summer . . . My
> problem is that I see both sides of every issue. I'm
> too logical. The world is not logical: if it was, old
> Gregor would not be younger than Young Gregor.

Though comically blunted by allusions to a Greek Fire Island, Boris's dilemma is that of a moral man in a perplexing
world. Like Yeats's "best," he lacks the conviction to insist
either that murder is always wrong, or that it is right under
extraordinary circumstances. And even if it were objectively
right, could his squeamish self subjectively handle it? *Love and
Death*'s unfulfilled assassination scene, with Boris wondering
how the Greeks would respond to his conflict, is paralleled in

Manhattan's lecture hall sequence, when Isaac demands that Yale defend his sluggish morality to upcoming generations. Both scenes are superficially outrageous: Isaac's pouting face is juxtaposed to the gleaming white skull of his skeletal ancestor, and Boris is pointing a gun at the collapsed false Napoleon. But Boris's dilemma is at once more real and more compelling. Where Isaac is clearly in the right, Boris vacillates between two half-wrongs. And the *Love and Death* resolution is more ruefully chastening, and finally truer. While Isaac huffs off in moral certitude (though he's lost the girl), irrational life has its way with Boris. Not only does someone else capriciously murder Napoleon, but Napoleon isn't Napoleon after all. So Boris dies for a crime he didn't commit, still undecided whether he ought to have committed it. As he suggested in his opening lines, this is the fate of all mankind—of artist and herring merchant, of the good as of the bad. And yet, Allen insists, there is a difference. Though he'll receive no thanks for his troubles, Boris was somehow the better for having scrutinized the nature of things.

Just as *Sleeper* anticipates the romantic format and cinematic inventiveness of *Annie Hall, Love and Death* anticipates *Annie Hall*'s greater depth and, further down the road, the moral conflicts in *Manhattan* and *Stardust Memories*. As the last and best of Allen's clearly nonbiographical comedies, it also stands a bit apart from the rest of his work—profoundly commenting on a world unencumbered by the specific personalities and New York situations of the upcoming films.

=6=

Sentimental Journey

Without Feathers,   *The Front,*
Annie Hall

Just as he branched out from his nightclub art in the mid-sixties, during the mid-seventies Allen explores various avenues of expression while concentrating most of his creative energy on filmmaking. His artistic and career choices become more aggressively serious. He does *not* make the vodka ad but breaks a policy of only performing in his own work to star in Martin Ritt's indictment of the McCarthy era, *The Front,* thus putting *Sleeper*'s moral lesson into practice. And the balance of his 1975 *Without Feathers*—short essays, stories, and plays—avoids the pithy *Getting Even* epigram in favor of sustained, more rueful comedy. With the 1977 *Annie Hall,* Allen at last discovers the serious theme to force his comic fragments into a meaningful whole.

Allen's conflicts—his vision of parallel trains, so to speak—are now midway between the comic indecision of Fielding Mellish and Sandy Bates's existential despair. Spelling out *Love and Death*'s comically insinuated inevitabilities, the best of these works are Allen's most pessimistic to date. Yet, as they portray appealing characters in realistic contemporary situations, they are his warmest and most involved as well. By stressing the cajolable mind over the anarchic body, "The Whore of Mensa" —among the best of the *Without Feathers* pieces—favors the personal give-and-take rather than the "scoring" aspect of love;

as does *Annie Hall,* where Alvy kisses Annie midway through their first date to "get that out of the way" so they can get on with the business of getting to like one another.

For while *Bananas, Sleeper,* and *Love and Death* were mostly about getting the girl, and *Manhattan* and *Stardust Memories* will be mostly about losing her (or them), *Annie Hall* is also about having and liking her. Significantly, the "fantasy" dispelled here is not that affection, but that romance, endures. Along with their endearing idiosyncrasies, the fact that Annie and Alvy never stop caring for one another is affectingly juxtaposed to the levelling reality that, in the words of a stranger Alvy consults on the street, "love fades."

Without Feathers

The title of Allen's second essay collection suggests a more involved humor than *Getting Even*'s. "How wrong Emily Dickinson was!" exclaims the narrator in the introductory essay. "Hope is not the thing with feathers. The thing with feathers has turned out to be my nephew. I must take him to a specialist in Zurich." Sometimes coy, often purposeful comic twists characterize the many diverse pieces in *Without Feathers.* And while they share the *Getting Even* parodic format, the best of these later works offer a more sustained comic narrative besides. "But Soft . . . Real Soft" (a spoof of the who-wrote-Shakespeare's plays controversy), for instance, shares "The Metterling Lists" 's irreverence for biographical scholarship. But where the earlier piece moves from funny observation to unrelated funny observation, "But Soft . . . Real Soft" is funny in parts and funnier still in its well-integrated entirety.

And while "The Metterling Lists" announces chaotic stylistic and theoretical inconsistencies at the start, "But Soft . . . Real Soft" more cunningly builds from a straightforward premise:

> Ask the average man who wrote the plays entitled *Hamlet, Romeo and Juliet, King Lear,* and *Othello,* and in most cases he'll snap confidently back with "The Immortal Bard of Stratford on Avon" . . . Now put these questions to certain literary detectives who

seem to crop up every now and again over the years,
and don't be surprised if you get answers like Sir
Francis Bacon, Ben Jonson, Queen Elizabeth and
possibly even the Homestead Act.

The twist to the increasingly preposterous exegesis which
follows is that it scrupulously hews to critical etiquette. Most
every "clue" from the opening paragraph is applied to the
ensuing argument. We are admonished not to confuse Ben
Jonson with Samuel Johnson: "He was Samuel Johnson. Sam-
uel Johnson was not. Samuel Johnson was Samuel Pepys . . ."
An apparently gratuitous allusion to "The Immortal Bard of
Stratford on Avon" pays off in a sentence which also embroils
Bacon, Marlowe, Alexander Pope, Pope Alexander, and Sir
Walter Raleigh:

> In an effort to conceal Marlowe from Shakespeare,
> should they prove to be the same person, Bacon had
> adopted the fictitious name Alexander Pope, who in
> reality was Pope Alexander, head of the Roman
> Catholic Church and currently in exile owing to the
> invasion of Italy by the Bards, last of the nomadic
> hordes (the Bards gave us the term "immortal
> bard"), who years before had galloped off to Lon-
> don, where Raleigh awaited death in the tower.

Why Raleigh? He was an "Elizabethan." And even evocation
of non-Elizabethan, non-poet George Eliot ("This all becomes
clearer when we realize George Eliot was a woman") "becomes
clearer" when we realize that a woman writing under male
pseudonym offers boundless opportunity for mistaken identity.

As with Dostoyevsky's titles in *Love and Death*'s prison
scene, the text's improbability is compounded by a subtextual
logic. While his pedant narrator strains for picayune analogies,
Allen intimates obvious literary and/or historical connections
between "buzz words" Shakespeare, Bacon, Marlowe, Jonson,
Pope, and even Queen Elizabeth. And while providing a comic
incongruity, the intelligence of the subtext also suggests an
alternative to abstruse erudition and, more insidiously, observes
that college drop-out Allen has a better grasp of his Shakespeare and company than many a card-carrying academic.

Like "The Moose," this essay is verbally as well as intellectually satisfying, with word play that enmeshes poetic references
and gibberish, and plot and theme twists which spiral toward
an apt, anti-climactic final quip:

> The point is, if you're going to move, notify your
> post office. Unless you don't give a hoot about pos-
> terity.

Just as "But Soft . . . Real Soft" is *Without Feathers's* denser
and more craftsmanly answer to "The Metterling Lists," "The
Whore of Mensa" is a more resonantly funny variation on "Mr.
Big," *Getting Even*'s shamus quest for the missing God. The
mystery is now sexual attraction. And where the final segment
of *Everything You Always Wanted to Know about Sex* takes a
sperm's and "Mission Control" view of intercourse, "The
Whore of Mensa" takes the cerebellum's part in the mind/body
conflict: if there are whores for the body, why not for the mind
as well? it demands. And why should one's intellectual desires
be limited by one's intellectual capacity? The lowly herring
merchant can yearn for otherness, the homely for the beautiful
mate: so why shouldn't an inarticulate mechanic named Word
Babcock lust above his IQ?

As Word presents his dilemma to shamus Kaiser:

> I'm a working guy . . . I build and service joy buzz-
> ers. You know—those little fun gimmicks that give
> people a shock when they shake hands? . . . I'm on
> the road a lot. You know how it is—lonely . . . Sure,
> a guy can meet all the bimbos he wants. But really
> brainy women—they're not so easy to find on short
> notice . . . I mean, my wife's great . . . But she won't
> discuss Pound with me.

So though Word loves his wife, he occasionally calls Flossie, a
"Madame with a masters in comparative lit," when he craves
"a quick intellectual experience." Now Flossie's threatening to
tell Word's wife. "Kaiser, you've got to help me," he implores.
"Carla would die if she knew she didn't turn me on up there."

All in the line of duty, Kaiser calls Flossie for a "girl" and
gets Melville expert Sherry: "a young redhead who was packed

into her slacks like two big scoops of ice cream" and whose pseudo-profundities have the ring of Sonia's in *Love and Death*. *Billy Budd,* for instance, is "Melville's justification of the ways of God to man, n'est-ce pas?" Kaiser can spot a phony when he hears one: "Whenever I offered an insight she faked a response." So once he's gotten his money's worth, Kaiser flashes his badge and threatens a bust if Sherry doesn't lead him to her Madame. She does. And after surviving a few surprises—Flossie is a college flunk-out, a man, and a lethal-weapon owner—Kaiser ties up the case.

As with "But Soft . . . Real Soft," "The Whore of Mensa" interweaves an increasingly ludicrous plot with a witty subtext, which here collides hard-nosed detective, New York intellectual, and sexual allusions. When the "girl" breaks under pressure, for instance, Kaiser muses:

> It all poured out—the whole story. Central Park
> West upbringing, socialist summer camps, Brandeis.
> She was every dame you saw waiting in line at the
> Elgin or Thalia . . . Only somewhere along the line
> she had made a wrong turn.

Flossie too made a "wrong turn" when, attempting to pass for Lionel Trilling, she "went to Mexico for an operation . . . I came out looking like Auden with Mary McCarthy's voice."

Where many of the earlier stories stress a discrepancy between altruistic or erudite pose and selfish or worthless goal, "The Whore of Mensa" notes a more endearing disparity between what Word is and what he finds stimulating. And beyond its superficial absurdity, Allen's parable drums home the logical point that a sharp intellect can be as sexually exciting and threatening as an enticing body. Yet all is not so logical or sanguine as it seems. The sexy intellectual "whores" are frauds; Word's physically appealing wife is boring; and, once he's solved the case, intellectual-surfeited Kaiser rushes off for dinner with a blond *cum laude* graduate: "The difference was she majored in physical education. It felt good." Thus "The Whore of Mensa" intimates what the later *Side Effects* stories will insist—that mental and physical provocation rarely turn up in the same person, and that the enigma of sexual arousal defies calculation.

Of the two one-act plays in *Without Feathers,* "God" takes
a one-note, self-parodic approach to the myth of free will in life
and art while "Death" seriously, and often soberly, evokes *Love
and Death*'s metaphysical questions in dramatic form. In this
latter, far better work, salesman Kleinman—like Nat Ackerman in the more broadly comic "Death Knocks"—is rudely
awakened to his mortality. A maniac strangler's on the prowl,
and at two A.M. one gloomy morning, a vigilante committee
demands Kleinman's participation in their manhunt. Kleinman
tries to demur gracefully: it's "the height of the season" and
"I'm not good at these things . . . Let me make a cash donation." But when his reticence provokes suspicion that Kleinman himself may be the maniac, he agrees to join and makes
anxious inquiries. What do the murder victims have in common? "There is no similarity," he is informed. "Except once
they all were alive and now they're dead." And mystery en-
shrouds the vigilantes' "plan" as well:

Kleinman:	So what do I do? What's my assign-ment?
Al:	If I were you I would try to contribute as best I could until my function be-came clearer.
Kleinman:	Contribute how?
Al:	It's hard to be specific.
Kleinman:	Can you give me a hint because I'm beginning to feel like a fool.
Al:	Things may seem chaotic, but they're not.

Although it's quickly apparent that the maniac is Death and
Kleinman's "assignment" his purpose in life, Allen sustains his
existential *Everyman* allegory with cool rather than parodic
humor and subtle plot twists. Convinced that his life depends
on discovering his "assignment," Kleinman furiously seeks out
knowledgeable company, but to little avail. A doctor with
scientific interest in the maniac suggests that Kleinman follow
him down a dark, dead-end alley. A young prostitute initiates
a discussion of infinitude and charges six dollars for a kiss. Soon
there are not one, but two obscure plans. And when Kleinman
again refuses to commit himself—"How can I choose when I

don't know the alternatives?"—both factions agree he's the
maniac. By the time the vigilantes appreciate their error, it's too
late for Kleinman, whose fatigued, Kleinman-like Maniac has
caught up with him. And while Ackerman outwitted Death,
Kleinman succumbs to his maniac, addressing a final quip to
mankind: "If there's life after death, and we all wind up in the
same place—don't call me, I'll call you."

"Death" is not without playfully comic interludes, such as a
discussion of reincarnation in which Kleinman observes, "Listen, anything's possible, but it's hard to imagine if a man is
president of a big corporation in this life, that he'll wind up as
a chipmunk." Yet, by exploiting suspense rather than humor to
thrust the plot forward, by conjuring an ominous tone and a
frequently unattractive protagonist, Allen here takes an important step toward his goal of serious drama.

"Death" is most provocative in contemplation of its hero and
his relationship to commitment and group endeavor. Where
Miles and Boris finally do their moral best in an unchangeable
world, Kleinman is sincere when he tells the prostitute, "I don't
want to get involved. I want to know what I'm supposed to be
doing." His self-oriented priorities never change, and yet plot
—and, by implication, life—developments show Kleinman in a
new light. The purportedly worthwhile "plan" is soon revealed
as vague and unstructured. The vigilantes who appeal to Kleinman's social conscience quickly desert him. And the very men
who band together for a common good at play's start fracture
and resort to capricious accusations at the end. In contrast to
both the play's other characters and to the conventional dramatic hero, Kleinman's attitude is consistent throughout. He's
unwilling to commit himself to a "plan" which endangers his
life at the outset and won't save his life by committing to one
of two similarly obscure "plans" at the end. Chance rather than
personal growth offsets Kleinman's inclinations as both logical
and courageous. As will be true in very different situations in
Annie Hall, Manhattan, and *Stardust Memories,* circumstance
makes a hero of a man who is equally a coward.

The Front

The not insignificant difference between Kleinman and Howard Prince, the Allen character in *The Front,* is that where the occasion flatters Kleinman, Prince rises to the occasion. There's not a touch of moral uncertainty in this characteristically high-minded Martin Ritt film: the insidious blacklisting policies of the McCarthy era are *The Front*'s unqualified evil. Walter Bernstein's script, written with Allen in mind, follows the pattern of Vittorio De Sica's *General della Rovere:* a weak man posing as a strong man winds up making a strong, disinterested gesture. Though sentimental, the premise is not unlikely; and McCarthyism, which tragically affected the public and personal lives of so many—among them Ritt, Bernstein, Zero Mostel, and a large percentage of *The Front*'s cast and crew—is a laudable occasion to rise to.

The Front is set in the early fifties, with the "Red Scare" on the rise in the entertainment industry as elsewhere. Its main characters are several black-listed writers, comic Hecky Brown (Zero Mostel), a well-meaning but spineless producer (Herschel Bernardi), his idealistic assistant Florence (Andrea Marcovicci), and "front" Howard Prince. Allen's presence permits a short-cut in Howard's character development. Although we meet him as night cashier in a bar, we have no trouble accepting that Howard, like Fielding and Miles before him, is a smart under-achiever who might attract successful friends like television writer Alfred Miller (Michael Murphy). In *The Front*'s first scenes, recently blacklisted Alfred asks Howard to perform as his "front"—e.g. to put his name to scripts Alfred will himself write. Since Howard's record is "clean" of communist associations, he'll have no trouble selling Alfred's scripts to the network and gleaning, Alfred assures him, a healthy share of lucrative profits. Welcoming the opportunity to simultaneously help a friend and himself, Howard readily agrees, as he will subsequently agree to "front" for several of Alfred's friends. Because his political credo is "look out for Number One," Howard doesn't care—indeed doesn't want to know—whether or not his "writers" are communist sympathizers.

As *The Front* rather predictably progresses, Harold, hailed as a humanitarian as well as a gifted scenarist, becomes a regular "writer" for the show on which Florence is assistant producer. Like Nancy in *Bananas,* Florence falls in love with a false impression of the Allen character; and she's appropriately grieved to discover that not only is he not a writer, but he takes the ostrich's perspective on human suffering. One after the other, the best network employees are threatened, fired, or ordered to spy on one another by a specious "loyalty" adviser, while Howard blithely goes about handing in his scripts and enjoying his new success. Inevitably, Howard himself is called for routine scrutiny by the House Un-American Activities Committee. Florence and Alfred beg him to take a stand. Although he's been jarred by the suicide of blacklisted comic Hecky Brown, Howard initially favors a compromise. Once before the committee, however, outrage makes a better man of him. "Fellas," he addresses the HUAC contingent, "I don't recognize the right of this committee to ask me these kinds of questions. And furthermore, you can go fuck yourselves." At last glimpse, Harold has one wrist in handcuffs and another around a beaming Florence—and the band plays on.

What's especially interesting about *The Front,* in light of Allen's career, is, first, his ability to evoke a Fielding Mellish sort of cunning underachiever, but now with a subtlety of expression (in contrast to Fielding's feverish mugging) which compellingly counterpoints the character's blatant flaws. The mutually respectful, almost tender relationship between broad, corpulent, older comic Mostel (Hecky) and understated, wiry newcomer Allen is affectingly evoked: even when Hecky unwillingly agrees to spy on Howard, there's no trace of established versus upstart comic's antagonism in either of their performances. The Michael Murphy–Allen relationship also merits note as it reverses the moral positions their characters will assume in *Manhattan.* At one point in *The Front,* Alfred tells Howard, "You know you're always looking for a middle you can dance around—this time there's no middle." Obviously Allen agrees, and thus takes time out from his own work to honor a worthy cause. Whatever its flaws, *The Front* is a worthy and finally moving tribute to and by those who suffered the evils of McCarthyism and would have us neither forget nor repeat them. But the absence of a "middle," so satisfying in life, is rarely the stuff of provocative drama, certainly not of Woody Allen's drama. Boris awkwardly poised over a false Napoleon is Woody Allen persona *and* artist; Howard Prince standing up to HUAC is Allen lending his support—not, as Kleinman would, with a "cash donation," but with the full, associational force of his person—to another man's admirable but less complicated vision of the world.

Annie Hall

As with *Play It Again, Sam* and *Everything You Always Wanted to Know about Sex* in the early seventies, Allen moved directly from his acting role in *The Front* into production on his own 1977 *Annie Hall.* And while *Annie Hall* is very much a Woody Allen film, it is not the film he set out to make. *Annie Hall*'s working title of *Anhedonia* is indicative of Allen's original intentions: scenes from the murder mystery script he abandoned for *Love and Death* would be interwoven with glimpses of problem childhood, career, and love experiences to the ends of portraying a successful, middle-aged man incapable of experiencing pleasure. At cutting-room stage, the story of Annie and Alvy was one of several equally stressed narrative components. But, as editor Ralph Rosenblum recalls, that story so insistently overwhelmed the others that *Annie Hall* was born. Discarded for the moment, *Anhedonia* will reemerge in *Stardust Memories.*

Social as well as artistic factors contributed to *Annie Hall*'s immediate success at the box office and its gleaning of four major Academy Awards. As was true with *City Lights* in the thirties, *The Best Years of Our Lives* in the post-war forties, *The Graduate* in the sixties, and *Five Easy Pieces* in the early seventies, *Annie Hall* touched a sensitive chord with contemporary audiences, and especially with well-educated, urban audiences. *Annie Hall*'s success is obliquely engaged in *Stardust Memories,* when Sandy Bates notes that his timing was "lucky." For Allen's bittersweet New York love story could not have arrived at a more propitious moment: by the late 1970s, many Americans had at least tentatively embraced feminism while rejecting the political optimism of the sixties, organized religion, and the heyday Hollywood portrait of happily-ever-after love. With

divorce rates rising, and career as an increasingly attractive
alternative to family—for women as well as men—audiences
could readily connect with a politically *and* romantically skeptical hero who nonetheless yearned for something wonderful as
an antidote to the depressing rituals of modern life.

As with Kleinman in "Death," events conspired to show
Alvy Singer's—and Woody Allen's—natural inclinations in fa-
vorable light. And yet while "lucky" timing may help account
for its initial popularity, *Annie Hall* has endured on artistic
merit. Stylistically, *Annie Hall* is Allen's most eclectic and
innovative film: exploiting split-screen, animation, instant re-
play, and visual stream-of-consciousness devices, introducing a
subtitled courtship interlude and several scenes of splintered
realism where Alvy leaves the confines of plot to mull over
events with his audience. Thematically, Allen's habitually fragmented narrative, as well as this stylistic eclecticism, now
makes compelling sense in light of *Annie Hall*'s kaleidoscopic
perception of modern life and its message that love dies, not
with a bang . . . Perhaps most important, *Annie Hall* makes
compelling use of a fifteen-year-old relationship between
Woody Allen—character, author, famous person—and his audience: this is our love story as well.

And *Annie Hall*'s monologue opening takes us back to the
start of our affair with Woody, before Diane existed and when
he was still a scruffy young stand-up comic. Now as then, he
comes to us with his love troubles. "Annie and I broke up,"
confesses a crestfallen Alvy Singer, who goes on to pose the
film's central question. What went wrong in the romance of
Alvy and Annie? Why did their—and by implication, why does
all—contemporary love die? And as we listen, the face of Alvy
Singer blurs, and we see the overlapping images of Woody
Allen: the artist Allen, for instance, who is now, like Alvy,
forty-two years old and a successful comedian; and the famous
Mr. Allen, who, again like Alvy, lived with Diane Keaton
(whose family name is Hall) for a while and is still her good
friend. Of course, and not unintentionally, there's a rub. Just as
Woody insisted "these things really happen to me" after the
most improbable nightclub monologue, Mr. Allen—in contemporary newspaper interviews—protests that this is *not* his and
Keaton's *real* story. But far from discouraging comparisons,

these protests intensify our curiosity and our emotional response. We are more interested in Alvy and Annie because they
may be Woody Allen and Diane Keaton; and we like Mr. Allen
and Ms. Keaton the better because they may be the lovable
Alvy and Annie.

And while thematic ramifications are complicated, the fact
that we know the plot's "Annie-and-I-broke-up" resolution
from the outset merely whets our interest in the story: because
we realize a love affair with Keaton will follow, we gladly
humor Alvy through a Brooklyn childhood and two unhappy
marriages. These early scenes, *Annie Hall*'s most chronological, are vital to narrative and, especially, character development. Child Alvy is father to the forty-year-old narrator, they
insist, in a shot of a small house quivering beneath a cartoon
roller coaster ("I was brought up under the roller coaster,"
Alvy explains), or in a scene where young Alvy exorcises his
frustrations on fellow bumper car drivers at Coney Island.

The boy who kisses outraged little girls because "I never had
a latency period" is Freudian ancestor to a sexually and otherwise confused adult who has "some trouble [differentiating]
between fantasy and reality." And Alvy's early metaphysical
depressions (he can't do his homework when he learns that "the
universe is everything," and it's shrinking), like those of Boris
before him, will be re-evoked in a scene where mature Alvy
buys Annie Ernest Becker's *Denial of Death* rather than a cat
book because "death is a big subject with me." Alvy's alienation
from adult society is similarly foreshadowed in a scene where
mature Alvy, like mature Virgil in *Take the Money and Run*'s
school band episode, assumes his child self's elementary school
chair and encourages former classmates to rise and declaim
their futures. "I run a profitable dress company," one small boy
smugly enunciates; another recites, "I used to be a heroin addict
—now I'm a methadone addict."

Between the Brooklyn episodes and glimpses of Alvy's two
marriages, Allen insinuates a few scenes between Annie and
Alvy at mid-affair: Annie arriving late at the Beekman movie
theater (this from the murder mystery script); Annie and Alvy
waiting on line to see *The Sorrow and the Pity;* a bedroom
discussion after the film. As well as assuring us that the love
affair will soon follow, these scenes ironically observe contempo-

rary mores. Reverence for the media, a familiar Allen absurdity, is spoofed as "the cast of *The Godfather*" hound Alvy for autographs because they saw him on the Johnny Carson show; and Alvy acknowledges the psychiatrist's crucial role as buttress to precarious modern love when he chastises Annie for sleeping through her psychiatrist appointment. By loudly alluding to "our sex problem" in public, Annie introduces the serious mind/body conflict in love but, more important here, epitomizes her decade's at once casual and overemphatic approach to sex.

In this segment's most imaginative gag, Annie and Alvy find themselves trapped beside a pompous Columbia University professor on the movie queue. After excoriating Fellini as "one of the most indulgent filmmakers," this *Getting Even* prototype moves on to the work of Marshall MacLuhan, at which point Allen takes pity on his exasperated persona. In a reality-fantasy segue as seamless as any in "The Great Renaldo," MacLuhan himself emerges from behind a billboard to chide: "You know nothing of my work . . . How you ever got to teach a course in anything is totally amazing." And the twist in Alvy's wistful, "Boy, if life were only like this . . ." response is that Alvy's resentment of the phony intellectual is, like Boris's, born of respect for legitimate art and thought.

In a later scene in which Annie and Alvy discuss *The Sorrow and the Pity* in bed (Annie: "It made me feel guilty"; Alvy: "It's supposed to."), Alvy's moral inclinations are established, and "our sex problem" is defined as Annie's recent disinclination to sleep with Alvy. Rather than illuminating, and thus stressing, Annie's particular trouble, Allen flashes back to sex problems in Alvy's past: with his first wife Allison (Carol Kane), for instance, where the disinclination was his. "Why did I turn off Allison Porschnik?" wonders an increasingly discriminating persona. Since Allison was bright, beautiful, and willing, Alvy suspects that the Groucho Marx "I'd never want to belong to any club that would have me as a member" joke applies.

A second flashback, more scathingly indicative of Woody's "the wife" routines, limns another sort of sex problem with Alvy's second New York Jewish intellectual wife, Robin (Janet Margolin, here barely recognizable as the laundress from *Take the Money and Run*). In a scene reminiscent of "The Whore of Mensa," intellectually ambitious Robin rushes Alvy into a party swarming with emissaries from *The New Yorker, The New York Review of Books, Commentary,* and *Dissent.* "I had heard *Commentary* and *Dissent* had merged and formed *Dysentery,* quips Alvy, who would prefer to eschew crabbed intellectual discussion in favor of straightforward physicality: watching the Knicks game on television and "quietly humping" with his wife. "The body never lies," argues Alvy, whose simple truth is counterpointed in the following scene by Robin's messy, neurotic, unsuccessful attempt to have an orgasm. She's taken Valium, been to a psychiatrist, her only hope is to move to the country. Could *Dysentery* be more complicated?

Annie Hall will further pursue the anomalies of sex as Annie's mind leaves her body during intercourse, and as Alvy labors to give Shelley Duvall's *Rolling Stone* reporter a "Kafka-esque" sexual experience. Yet, where Allen's later films dwell on the inexorable antagonism between mind and body, *Annie Hall* more comically observes how a purportedly spontaneous pleasure can tax the mind and emotions. Through Allison and Robin, Allen blunts the thematic relevance of Annie's sexual idiosyncrasies—her need for a relaxing "joint" before sex and, later, her loss of sexual appetite. More important, these sober intellectuals felicitously offset Annie's shy exuberance. After a few scenes with Alvy's ex-wives, our response to his meeting Annie is not unlike Kaiser's "It felt good" reaction to the physical education *cum laude* at the end of "The Whore of Mensa," which is, of course, Allen's intention. During Annie and Alvy's courtship scenes, situated a third of the way into the film, Allen briefly ignores the darker aspects of romance and revels in a never sharper or warmer tension between Keaton and himself.

Annie and Alvy's courtship scenes reverse roles established in *Play It Again, Sam.* At their first meeting, after a tennis match, it's he who's socially and physically adept (she compliments him on his tennis game), while she struggles with flailing hands and legs, barely escapes multiple collisions as she drives home through the New York streets, and can't divine a graceful means of prolonging their acquaintance. Still, for all her gaucheries and self-effacing "oh-la-dee-dahs," Annie's sparkling face and bold, awkward motions convey intuition and curiosity about life; and, like Allan Felix, she's discriminating, as a first dialogue (with subtitles conveying the characters' thoughts) reveals. Allen sets this scene on Annie's terrace. "You're what Grammy Hall would call a real Jew," Annie tells Alvy, who repays the compliment by praising her photographs:

> *Alvy:*   They're wonderful, you know. They have a quality.
> *sub:*   You are a great-looking girl.
> *Annie:* Well, I would like to take a serious photography course.
> *sub:*   He probably thinks I'm a yo-yo.
> *Alvy:*   Photography's interesting because it's a new form, and a set of aesthetic criteria have not emerged yet.
> *sub:*   I wonder what she looks like naked . . .

And a bit later:

> *Alvy:*   The medium enters in as a condition of the art form itself.
> *sub:*   I don't know what I'm saying—she senses I'm shallow.
> *Annie:* To me, ah, it's all instinctive. You know, I just try to get a sense of it and not think so much . . .
> *sub:*   God, I hope he doesn't turn out to be a schmuck like the others.

Inspiredly reconceiving the foreign film subtitle (and intimating that courtship is indeed an exotic tongue), this scene evokes the absurdity, but also the excitement, of romantic attraction and captures a truth about all courtships without diminishing the singularity of Annie and Alvy's. And Allen sustains this balance between the particular and the universal as Alvy, the famous New York comedian, and Annie, the novice Midwestern singer, get to know one another: during their first date when she sings well, but hesitantly, to a restless audience; in the bookstore where he buys her *Denial of Death* and praises education; at a summer house in the Hamptons where Annie and Alvy chase their live lobster dinner around the kitchen and Alvy suggests luring the strayed beast with hot butter sauce.

With many of Alvy's implacable likes and dislikes established, these scenes concentrate on Annie's more susceptible nature: flashing back to shots of her with a blank-faced, gum-chomping Chippewa Falls high school beau, and then with a more recent, intense actor lover of the Erno mold. Where Alvy, we have discovered, is wary of strangers, passionately attached to New York (for him, California's only "cultural advantage" is that "you can turn right on a red light"), and more than a little anhedonic (unable to have a good time); Annie is adventurous, unpredictable, and stimulated by new experiences. Yet, in these early scenes, Annie and Alvy's differences are mutually attracting, and their happiness is at once special and indicative of happy love the world over.

And Tolstoy notwithstanding, Annie and Alvy's unhappiness is also that of all unhappy couples. What is *cinematically* novel here is that boundaries between happiness and unhappiness are purposefully obscured. We're shown no first time that Annie doesn't want to sleep with Alvy, no morning when Alvy awakes to discover that Annie's once endearing volatility has grown annoying. Where the traditional Hollywood romance posits a specific when and why (the other woman in *The Awful Truth,* crossed purposes in *Adam's Rib,* an unearthed secret in *The Graduate*) things "go wrong," this is not so comfortably the case here. By fragmenting plot and skewing chronology, by showing us Annie and Alvy bickering before their first kiss, Allen undermines the salience of a pivotal event and underscores the depressing perspicacity of a stranger's advice to Alvy. "It's never something you did. That's how people are. Love fades."

And, in keeping with its fragmented style, *Annie Hall* continues to scrutinize the mystery of "love fades" in terms, not of one, but of many overlapping conflicts. As in *Sleeper,* those conflicts are often between enduring love and contemporary society: juxtaposing the difficulty of building a life with one person to the ease of discovering attractive alternatives. Annie's increasingly successful singing career wins her admirers more lively and less demanding than Alvy. After a Beverly Hills party, Alvy realizes that "it's fun to flirt." Why should he endure "the usual problems in bed tonight with Annie"?

Again as in *Sleeper,* the tension between emotional need and the metaphorical "chemical in our bodies that makes it so we all

get on each others' nerves" is well delineated here. Annie and
Alvy have their very particular grievances and eccentricities. Though grateful for his help (Alvy pays for Annie's psychiatrist and encourages her career), Annie resents her indebtedness
to Alvy and finds him morose and unadventurous. When he
sniffs cocaine, it's only (hysterically) to sniff $2,000 worth into
the air. "You like those New York girls" and "You don't think
I'm smart enough to take seriously" are also frequent complaints. For his part, Alvy suffers the persona's familiar ambivalence about commitment. Annie should live with him but retain
her $400-a-month, bug-ridden apartment as a "life raft" to
assure them they're not married. And after wheedling a first
confession of love from Annie, Alvy, like Fielding in *Bananas,*
vertiginously circles the issue: "love" is too weak a word; he
"lurvs," he "loavs," he "luffs," he will not say, "I love you."

   Those who insist that *Annie Hall* is about the simultaneous
attraction and incompatibility of opposites find their point vividly argued in two split-screen sequences (shot by cinematogra-
pher Gordon Willis in this first of many fruitful collaborations
with Allen). The first of these scenes evolves as the "real Jew"
sits down to a Chippewa Falls Easter dinner with Annie's Pres-
byterian family. Feeling no more comfortable than the Berkowitz "moose" on the wall of the City Athletic Club, Alvy lets
his mind wander toward a comic juxtaposition. We see Alvy's
perception of Annie's versus his own heritage: on one side of
the screen, the genteel Halls drink, demurely pick at their ham
dinner, and discuss alcoholic friends and 4-H Club meetings; on
the other side, the Singer family gathers around the seltzer
bottle and gorges on everything *but* ham, while one-upping
each other with tales of fulsome illnesses, deaths, and, worse
still, unemployment. *Annie Hall*'s second split-screen sequence
simultaneously observes Annie and Alvy with their respective
psychiatrists. When asked the same question—"Do you have
sex often?"—Alvy replies, "Hardly ever, maybe three times a
week"; while Annie sighs, "Constantly, I'd say three times a
week." The opposition motif is carried a step further in an
animation sequence where Alvy envisions Annie as the wicked
stepmother he preferred to Snow White in the Disney cartoon:
even as a child, Alvy grumbles, he was perversely attracted to
the troubled "other."

And yet, as with all Allen's most provocative conflicts, Annie's and Alvy's opposition can be just as convincingly refuted—stylistically and narratively. Like Miles and Luna in *Sleeper,* and Boris and Sonia in *Love and Death,* Annie and Alvy are the only two visually full-bodied characters in *Annie Hall*'s more realistic world of cartoon prototypes: Shelley Duvall's fashionably mystical *Rolling Stone* reporter; the guest who calls home from a Beverly Hills party because "I forgot my mantra"; the tailored, vapidly smiling New York couple who reveal the secret of their happiness:

> *Woman:*   I'm very shallow, and I have no ideas
> and nothing to say.
> *Man:*   And I'm exactly the same.

Allen discovers a visual correlative for Alvy's spontaneous, off-beat humor in Annie's unselfconsciously distinctive, eclectic costuming—baggy pants, vest, tie, hat, tear-shaped glasses. And if Annie and Alvy are opposites, what can be said of the mates they select after the break-up: Annie's glib, unperturbable L.A. record producer, Tony Lacey (Paul Simon), and the sophisticated New Yorker who won't chase lobsters with Alvy in the Hamptons?

Even toward the end of the film, when relations are more consistently testy, for almost every scene which observes Annie and Alvy implacably at odds, there's another which attests to their romantic rightness. Their false crises and reconcilations, which at once parody and exploit romantic comedy conventions, are indicative. An initial break-up, for instance, is precipitated by suspected infidelity. Having touted adult education as "a wonderful thing, you meet a lot of interesting professors," Alvy discovers Annie arm-in-arm with one such creature and is enraged. Significantly, it's the suspect now rather than the offended party who breaks relations: though he won't commit himself, Alvy's "spying on me!" wails Annie, who retreats to the "life raft."

She's right, he's right, their parting is inevitable. Yet, as will be true to the final, self-conflicted scene, there's a "yes, but": a following sequence where the *very* false crisis of a bug in Annie's bathroom brings Alvy to the rescue and reconciliation at two

A.M.; a pleasurable outing to Alvy's "old neighborhood" in Brooklyn; Alvy's birthday packages for Annie—a flashy, low-cut red nightgown (Annie: "That's for you!") and the watch she's wanted. And while the upcoming Mary, of *Manhattan,* and Dorrie, in *Stardust Memories,* will be, by turns, morally and psychologically abrasive to a persona clearly stimulated by antagonism, there's far more than irrational, self-destructive attraction between Annie and Alvy. One very lovely shot of Annie at the microphone captures the peculiar intimacy and uncompetitive caring of their relationship. This shot is situated near the end of the film. As on Annie and Alvy's first date (which Annie's "Seems Like Old Times" song selection acknowledges), Annie is singing in a nightclub, but now her demeanor is assured, and her audience is hushed and appreciative. A visual valentine, this sustained image gleans resonance from art/life ambivalence—is this Alvy or Allen or both saluting Annie/Keaton? In any case, a good deal more than perverse opposition is at work.

Annie Hall does, however, introduce one straightforward opposition in its sub-plot conflict between Alvy's beloved New York and California, defended by his best friend Rob (again played by Tony Roberts). After much convincing, Alvy and Annie agree to let Rob guide them through the L.A. sunshine, canned laughter television studios, award dinners, and to a Beverly Hills party where successive executives agree to "take a meeting," until one observes, "All the good meetings are taken." California precipitates the "false" climax of Annie and Alvy's final break-up. While Annie enjoys Los Angeles' balmy, relaxed climate, Alvy adheres to his earlier statement that, "When I get mellow, I ripen and rot." And on the plane ride home, they calmly agree that a relationship is, in Alvy's words, "like a shark—if it doesn't go *constantly* forward it dies," and "What we have on our hands is a dead shark."

Like its opening, *Annie Hall*'s concluding scenes move swiftly and chronologically. In keeping with the film's tone, Annie's packing is, but for a Christmas tree in the background, devoid of sentimental detail. The palaver is very much as usual, with Alvy paranoidly insisting that Annie wrote her name in his favorite books because "you knew this day was gonna come," and she magnanimously leaving any book with "death" in its title. Even as they assure one another that nothing's permanent, that they can come back together as they have in the past, Annie looks relieved to be off. So we're not surprised that when, a few months later, Alvy discovers "I made a terrible mistake!" and stoops to visiting Annie in Los Angeles and proposing marriage, she is no longer so eager to be "taken seriously." Now the tables are turned: it's she who won't say she loves him or even agree to return to New York, while he's insecurely out of his element and yearning for commitment. As befits a former bumper-car crasher, Alvy throws a motorized temper tantrum, which lands him in jail, while the suntanned Annie accompanies her record producer housemate to the Grammy Awards.

So, as Alvy asks in his opening monologue, what happened? Why did/does love fade? On the one hand, as previously observed, the reasons are aggregate and often timely, ranging from Annie's growing independence and interest in her career to Alvy's yen to "flirt" and have better sex. But, on the other hand, Alvy's question is the flip side of wondering why Irene Dunne and Cary Grant put infidelity aside and get back to their marriage at the end of *The Awful Truth;* or why lawyers Hepburn and Tracy sweep their competitive wills under the bed in *Adam's Rib.* Certainly Annie and Alvy have problems, but they would not have spelled "dead shark" in a typical thirties or forties, or even a fifties or sixties romantic comedy. They would have been confronted and elaborated upon in crisis after crisis in the film's first hour and then have vanished or been made to seem trivial in light of the couple's shared affection, experience, and a far more troubling prospect of separation.

Not surprisingly, the wistful final scene of *Annie Hall* recalls the *narratively* very different resolutions to these earlier films: for both imply compromise and loss. By coming back together, having acknowledged their problems and differences, Tracy and Hepburn and Dunne and Grant suggest that there is no such thing as "perfect love": that their imperfect affection is the finest that is to be found in this far from best of all possible worlds. With Annie and Alvy, the opposite is true. Beyond the hard, social, unromantic half-truths about their break-up, there's a level on which Annie, Alvy, and Allen are, not less, but more romantic than their predecessors. Annie and Alvy part because they have social options Hepburn and Tracy didn't have; but also because, despite their pragmatic talk of "sharks" and "relationships," each is still in search of the fantasy Tracy and Hepburn acknowledged as impossible: the "perfect romance," symbolized by good sex, but actually something far more elusive.

Despite its timely details, *Annie Hall* is fundamentally neither timely nor realistic. In sharp contrast to such contemporary works as Michael Ritchie's 1977 *Semi-Tough*, Paul Mazursky's 1978 *An Unmarried Woman*, and Claudia Weill's 1978 *Girlfriends*, Allen observes but never stresses current social issues: never posits feminism (any more than as a narrative crisis), for instance, as "the reason why" something does or doesn't happen between a man and a woman. Where Mazursky's and Weill's respective "unmarried" heroines temporarily eschew romantic commitment in favor of "self-fulfillment," Annie and Alvy immediately take on new mates. Where *Semi-Tough*'s two-time loser in the marriage of opposites must lose yet another "opposite" mate to learn the value of friendship in love, Annie and Alvy are always friends.

Though it focuses on successful, romantically experienced adults in their thirties and forties, *Annie Hall* is really about first love and, in a curious way, about childhood. The memory images which flash through Alvy's mind at film's end—Annie and Alvy at the Hamptons, Annie and Alvy in Brooklyn, Annie and Alvy pointing out to sea—are snapshots from an unreasonably hopeful past, intellectually, but never emotionally, outgrown. Alvy's final speech perfectly encapsulates this tension:

> It was great seeing Annie again. I realized what a terrific person she was, and how much fun it was just knowing her. And I thought of that old joke: You know, this guy goes to a psychiatrist and says, "Doc, my brother's crazy. He thinks he's a chicken." And the doctor says, "Well, why don't you turn him in?" And the guy says, "I would, but I need the eggs." Well, I guess that is pretty much the way I feel about relationships. You know, they're totally irrational and absurd, but I guess we keep going through it, because most of us need the eggs.

Allen's most pessimistic film thus far is also his most romantic.

In *What's New, Pussycat?*, his first film for Charles Feldman, Woody can't summon up the nerve to defend his beloved Carol's (Romy Schneider's) book from an aggressive reader.

As would-be criminal Virgil Starkwell in *Take the Money And Run,* Woody fashions a "magic" gun out of a bar of soap and shoe polish. (And then "real" rain turns his escape weapon to soap bubbles . . .)

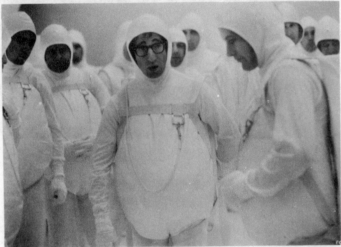

Woody flourishes a smiling moppet version of himself as he insults the king in the first section of *Everything You Always Wanted to Know About Sex*.

In *Everything You Always Wanted to Know About Sex*'s last and best section, Woody plays a space-age sperm timidly awaiting take-off.

Woody and Louise Lasser play lovers in *Bananas*. Although he insists, "I loveya," she perceives that "something's missing" between them.

The "something" that was missing between Louise Lasser and Woody in *Bananas* —namely movie chemistry—is very much in evidence when Linda Christie (Diane Keaton) and Allan Felix (Woody) come together in the 1972 film version of *Play It Again, Sam* (directed by Herbert Ross).

Woody plays the only robot with glasses and moral indignation in *Sleeper* society.

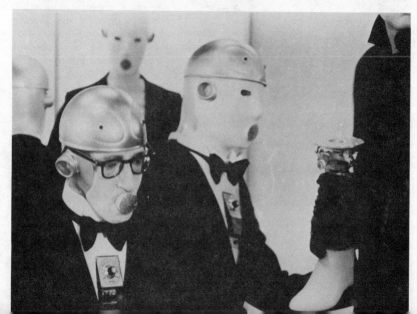

In *Love and Death,* Boris and Sonia (Woody and Keaton) face a truly provocative moral dilemma: to murder or not to murder the (false) Napoleon, played by James Tolkan.

With a bow to Ingmar Bergman and Bob Hope, Boris "contends with" and loses out to the great mystery of death.

The Front conveys a mutually respectful, almost tender relationship between the broad, older comic Zero Mostel (as Hecky) and Woody, playing "front" Howard Prince.

Alvy Singer's (Woody's) adult alienation is foreshadowed in an early scene in *Annie Hall*, where the mature Alvy assumes his child self's spot in the elementary school room.

Differences between Annie (Keaton), the loveable Midwestern eccentric, and Alvy (Woody), a New York neurotic, are suggested in split-screen sequences such as the above. (Humphrey Davis plays Alvy's psychiatrist.)

Still, incompatabilities notwithstanding, *Annie Hall* finds the Allen-Keaton chemistry at its warmest and most compelling.

Interiors' Chekhovian family tensions—notably, between sisters Joey (Mary Beth Hurt) and Renata (Keaton)—are as complicated as those parodied in *Love and Death*.

Though its tone is often sardonic, *Manhattan*'s black-and-white images—
such as the above silhouette of Woody and Keaton—are luminous.

It's not by chance that Isaac (Woody) is, in his words, "winner of the August
Strindberg Award" when "it comes to relationships with women": in this
affectionate scene at a soda fountain, he prepares to leave the loveable Tracy
(Mariel Hemingway) for neurotic Mary (Keaton).

At the opening of *Stardust Memories,* we see Sandy Bates (Woody) in the "wrong" train, filled with grotesque, inexplicably anguished people.

Though he knows the "perfect woman" doesn't exist, Sandy is still looking for the "eggs" of happily-ever-after romance—here with the beautiful, schizophrenic Dorrie (Charlotte Rampling).

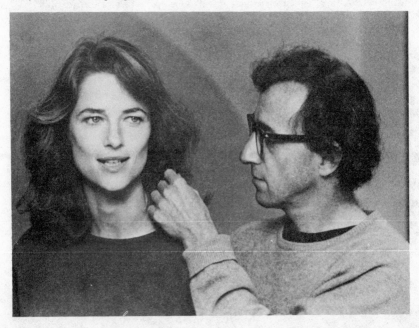

=7=

Tunnel Vision

Interiors,   Manhattan

In the spring of 1978, the American Academy of Motion Picture Arts and Sciences awarded *Annie Hall* Best Picture, Best Director, Best Original Screenplay (an honor Allen shares with co-writer Marshall Brickman), and a Best Actress award for Diane Keaton, while, in the spirit of Alvy Singer, its creator was home in bed. The success of this fullest and most conspicuously serious of his films gave Allen the confidence and prestige to embark on his long-cherished ambition of creating serious drama: "plunging in," he recalls, "not with a ganster film or melodrama, but with what I consider real drama of the hardest kind, where conflicts are small and hopefully seething and complicated." Yet the autobiographical texture and sheer breadth of ideas explored in *Annie Hall* brought Allen creative difficulties as well: having already wrung a wealth of themes from personal experience, where does the self-oriented artist now turn? Could Allen say any more on his thus far most compelling topics of contemporary society and love—and if so, how?

Though neither film is thoroughly successful, *Interiors* and *Manhattan* present ambitious alternatives: with *Interiors,* Allen leaves comedy, persona, and personal experience behind to penetrate the unfamiliar world of a repressed New York Wasp family in terms of Ingmar Bergmanesque drama; with *Manhattan,* he resumes a comic format while insinuating increasingly tragic ideas and characterizations. Both films introduce prominent sub-plots and put Gordon Willis's suggestive cinematography to thematic use. "Just as I often write scenes with Diane Keaton's talents in mind," says Allen, "in *Interiors, Manhattan,* and *Stardust Memories,* I began creating situations hospitable to Gordon Willis's sensibility. I know the way he thinks, and I try to give him something he can go with."

Allen's scope has now expanded: the world is no longer comprised of cartoons offsetting a single, full-bodied romantic couple, but is visually and narratively multiplicitous. And while love remains a central issue in both films, nuances of family relationships and friendship are increasingly engaged. *Interiors* introduces the possibility of suicide—not, as was comically the case with Woody's mother, because a son alludes to divorce— but because a husband insists on it. *Manhattan* takes solemn issue with the axiomatic "All's fair in love and war." And each film presses beyond traditional romantic comedy to explore the new terrain of middle-aged courtship in *Interiors* and a lesbian household and a middle-aged man's affair with a seventeen-year-old girl in *Manhattan.*

"Talent is luck. The important thing in life is courage," pronounces Isaac at the beginning of *Manhattan.* And both films probe society's quite different, and to Allen's mind reprehensible, verdict on the relative value of good art and admirable behavior. Though Joey is *Interiors*'s braver and more generous daughter, Renata's greater talents win her a favored position with their mother, as with the world at large. Though Isaac puts friendship before infatuation—courting Mary only when she's broken with his best friend Yale—he receives no such consideration when the tables are turned. Much as *Sleeper* and *Annie Hall* wonder how love can endure in a society intoxicated by change, *Interiors* and *Manhattan* question the possibility of romantic integrity in a world indifferent to ethical standards. Through its single virtuous character, seventeen-year-old Tracy (Mariel Hemingway), *Manhattan* stretches this problem a metaphysical point further to confront the purity of youth with inevitable corruption.

And, as in *Love and Death,* Allen's moral messages are counterpointed by more resonant uncertainties: what is the responsible course of action when one prefers a new lover to a still dependent current mate (a problem for Arthur in *Interiors* and Isaac in *Manhattan*)? Or, to what extent is the grown child obliged to indulge a scornful, but also needy, nervously unbalanced parent (Joey's dilemma in *Interiors*)?

There's a troubling creator/character inconsistency in both these films: between prodigious artist Allen and prototypes who seem to glean little satisfaction from accomplishment. Reasonably, Allen, Isaac, and Renata would all still prefer to achieve immortality through "not dying." But with this scarcely an option, Allen, in the late seventies, continues to turn out film after story after short play, while his most sympathetic characters spend a good deal of time deploring bad art (such as the television show Isaac quits) and others' wasted talents. Alvy buys Annie *Denial of Death,* Ernest Becker's argument for accomplishment as psychological release from the dread of death. Renata reprimands her often slothful husband, "I turn things out!" And Isaac invokes Yale's failure to complete his long-contemplated biography of Eugene O'Neill as indicative of moral torpor. But what of the *virtues* of artistic endeavor, of the creative act as logical bridge between the "luck" of talent and the struggle of moral courage? Is Becker right or isn't he when he describes accomplishment as a profound release? And if he *is* right, then why does Isaac spend no more time at work than Fielding? Why, in a final scene in *Manhattan,* does this quite realistic persona cite symphonies and novels and "Tracy's face," but not the act of creating as compensation for life's disappointments? Since *Interiors* and *Manhattan* are both quests for a reason to go on living, Allen's failure to grapple with the option of work upsets the thematic balance in films which are otherwise among Allen's most polished and considered.

Interiors

Allen found the uninterrupted seriousness of *Interiors* more difficult, but also more rewarding than comedy, even the mixed comedy and seriousness of *Manhattan* and *Stardust Memories.* "What so many people don't understand," he observed to this writer, in the tone of Isaac Singer or Sandy Bates, "is that

comedy is impossible if you can't do it, but it's no big deal if
you can—it's just good luck. I can sit down in an afternoon and
do a couple of pages for the *New Yorker* and start a script and
write some jokes. If I'm on the film set and I have to revise a
scene to make it funny, that's easy for me. But revising *Interiors*
was very, very difficult. I was in completely unfamiliar waters."

And as when confronted with the unfamiliar challenges of
writing first nightclub acts, plays, stories, and comic films,
Allen turned unapologetically to admired models—now specifically to the works of Chekhov, Shakespeare, and Ingmar Bergman. *Interiors* opens with cuts from a pale Long Island beach
house to a starkly furnished New York office building, setting
the visual and emotional mood for the piece which follows. As
at the start of *Annie Hall,* a narrator directly addresses his
audience: but now confiding analysand Alvy is supplanted by
sorrowful, hesitant Arthur, a sixty-year-old man who might be
defending himself to judge and jury. Arthur evokes an image
of his estranged wife Eve:

> I had dropped out of law school when I met Eve. She
> was very beautiful—very pale and cool in her black
> dress, without anything more than a simple strand
> of pearls—and distant . . . At the time the girls were
> born, it was all so perfect—so ordered. Looking
> back, of course, it was rigid. It was like an ice castle.

The "girls" Arthur alludes to are his and Eve's now grown-
up daughters: Renata (Diane Keaton), a famous poetess; Joey
(Mary Beth Hurt), an intelligent but artistically ungifted middle child; and television actress Flynn (Kristin Griffith). As in
King Lear, The Three Sisters, and *Cries and Whispers,* these
sisters are galvanized by what is, for them, extraordinary
events: after years as dutiful husband, Arthur requests a "tem-
porary separation" from Eve and leaves to vacation in Greece.
Not for the first time, Eve suffers a nervous breakdown and, as
the film gets underway, slowly recovers, moves from Long
Island to a New York apartment, and takes steps toward
resuming an interior decorating career by reshaping her daughter Joey's apartment.

Our sympathies are immediately with Arthur and the often disgruntled Joey. Despite physical and emotional frailties, Eve is manifestly willful and domineering. And with Flynn in Hollywood and authoress Renata ensconced in Connecticut, New Yorker Joey bears the thankless burden of amusing and undeceiving her mother. "It's only a trial separation," cajole Renata and Flynn from afar. But Joey's more discouraging forecast proves correct; and Arthur returns from Greece, determined to leave the "ice castle" and remarry a demonstrative, artless woman named Pearl—in Joey's opinion, "a vulgarian." While precipitating Eve's suicide, the ensuing marriage and its aftermath also ring changes on other family members, and notably on Joey.

Interiors' Chekhovian family tensions are as complicated as those parodied in *Love and Death:* Renata is married to a once-promising novelist, Frederich (Richard Jordan), who vents recent literary frustrations in alcoholic rage and vituperative *New York Times* book reviews. Grudgingly respectful of his productive wife, Frederich is sexually attracted to the glamorous Flynn, whom he compares to his latest book: "a perfect example of form without content." Though Renata encourages her husband, she haughtily dismisses Joey's earnest creative endeavors: "She has all the anxiety of the artistic personality without any of the talent." And, still searching for an art at which she can excel, Joey refuses to commit herself to a skein of unfulfilling office jobs or to her solicitous political filmmaker mate, Mike (Sam Waterston). Eve favors Renata, who, in Joey's words, "doesn't give you the time of day," while Arthur lavishes affection on a similarly unresponsive Joey.

At once literally and symbolically allusive, *Interiors'* title refers to Eve's interior decorating profession and to most of the characters' self-consciously inner preoccupations. More obliquely, it suggests Eve's preference for the manageable indoors and anticipates a mythic confrontation between herself and the chaotic "exterior" force of the ocean—both Jungian subconscious and deep blue sea—in the film's climax. And similarly Allen's "three sisters" are at once avatars and idiosyncratic, often spiteful flesh-and-blood. In Allen's early comedies he swiftly delineates protagonists and satirical targets, but in *Interiors* he portrays Renata, Joey, and (less successfully) Flynn as at once maddeningly flawed and sympathetic.

In Keaton's powerful, humorless performance, Renata evolves as an unengagingly strident woman, jealous of her time and family position and, though superficially concerned, deeply indifferent to a failed artist husband and to the pretty young daughter she seems to be rearing for show. And yet it is through Renata that Allen conveys very personal feelings about the act of creation. In one sustained close-up, we watch her irascibly, drearily pencilling, crossing out, and rewriting a phrase (purportedly Allen's writing method as well); and there's a chilling, if stilted, moment when Renata walks dazedly from her work to tell her husband, "I felt precarious, like I was a machine that was functioning, but that I could konk out at any second." Without Alvy Singer's release of humor, Renata is constantly oppressed by thoughts of death. Like Eve, Renata fastidiously decorates her home and unswervingly follows routine (she won't miss an arranged party, for instance, when her depressed husband longs to stay home) in hopes of deflecting mortality. Yet, because Renata is also striving to perfect her artistic talents, daughter's predilections are less abrasive than mother's.

Where *Annie Hall*'s narrative fragments often take their rhythm from comic incidents, *Interiors'* similarly episodic early scenes briefly glimpse indicative dramatic moments, often noting concept/reality or figurative/literal conflicts: Renata discussing "feelings of futility in relation to my work" with her psychiatrist, and later shopping in a fashionable boutique with Frederich; Joey sensitively musing, "I feel a real need to express something, but I don't know what it is I want to express," and, upon learning she's pregnant, angrily snapping at Mike's suggestion that she have the baby. Though Joey's creative dilemma is the most pressing, before Pearl bursts on the scene, Eve is uncontestibly *Interiors'* dramatic center, and Allen takes great visual pains observing her: regally entering Joey's apartment, bearing a pale, extravagant vase she's spotted at an auction; sealing her beige kitchen with thick black masking tape for a first suicide attempt. Annie's eclectic clothing reveals personal spontaneity, whereas Eve's labored tastefulness and simplicity —the pale vase, the "strand of pearls" Arthur recalls—convey not only aesthetic discretion, but a tenacious aversion to chance and effulgence.

Interiors' cinematography is purposely self-conscious and often unabashedly metaphorical: a tightly framed, sustained shot of Eve and Joey in an opening scene underscores their *"huit clos"* relationship; an image emphasizing Eve, Renata, and Joey's descending order of physical grandeur clearly has family hierarchy on its mind as well. An opening scene at the Long Island house portrays Joey and Renata—each looking out the beach-front window—in separate shots; a final sequence, after Eve's funeral, shows all three daughters at the same window together.

Though its plot developments are mostly chronological, its characters visually full-bodied, *Interiors* looks no more credibly real than do *Sleeper* and *Love and Death.* Where these comedies embellish the world, *Interiors'* muted pastel summer and winter homes and bland lands and seascapes are distillations of real life, a bleached version of *Sleeper's* bright pinks and blues. *Interiors'* verbal canvas is similarly unnatural, and there's a deracinated quality to dialogue, such as Renata's "It is as if I had a clear vision where everything seemed sort of awful and predatory", or Joey's "At the center of a sick psyche, there is a sick spirit."

At their least effective, *Interiors'* expository scenes merely exploit character as vessel for ideas; but at their frequent best, they develop themes through characters who are as complex as they are complicated. The influence of *King Lear* is provocatively felt in sequences where Eve, accustomed to power, persists on a verbally authoritative course even when events are clearly out of her control. And initially Joey's scrupulous honesty with her mother is presented in Cordelia-like opposition to Renata and Flynn's facile reassurances. At Eve's birthday celebration, for instance, the camera isolates Joey as her two sisters rush to console their weeping mother that "everything'll work out" with Arthur. Significantly, when Joey walks into the frame, the back of her head obscures her sister's disingenuously comforting faces.

Yet soon Allen invests Joey's fierce integrity and seeming selflessness with darker motives. Uncertain in her own goals—

unable to decide whether or not to marry Mike, to abort the
baby, to take the job with this advertising agency or that story
department—Joey is as psychologically dependent on her
mother's albeit exasperating needs as her mother is on the
generosity of this least favorite of her daughters. Through
Joey's resistance both to Mike ("Why do you stay with me?
. . . I give you nothing but grief," she aptly informs him) and
to the father who so obviously favors her, Allen evokes Alvy
Singer's "I wouldn't want to belong to any club . . . ," now on
a family level as well. More insistently than in the comedies,
Allen notices the petty grudges, jealousies, and preferences that
complicate relationships. Renata takes unmistakable glee in
peremptorily dismissing Joey's photographs as mediocre and
bemoaning, "Naturally, I'm put in the position of having to
encourage her." Joey displays a mixture of pride and envy at
her older sister's success, observing, "I read something of yours
in a magazine . . . It was very beautiful." And even when his
wife's in the hospital, Arthur can't hide his greater preoccupation with Joey, confiding in an exasperated Renata, "She has no
direction. I expected such great things from her."

Although, as previously noted, *Interiors* fails to grapple with
the rewards of hard work, its comments on art are often insightful. As with Metterling's books versus Metterling's life, Allen's
juxtaposition of Renata the gifted poetess and Renata the wanting human being drives home the discrepancy between creation
and creator. And life and art are similarly opposed as Eve's
preoccupation with perfect color schemes and spatial arrange-
ments robs her, and her offspring, of unpremeditated experience. Renata's complaints to her psychiatrist ("Why am I
striving to create, anyway?") convey Allen's oft-repeated conviction that "art doesn't save you. The sense of being immortal
through your work is as illusory as the Catholic idea of an
afterlife and a heaven." Most movingly, through Joey's struggle
to achieve "fantasy" release through creating, *Interiors* observes the frustrations of a fertile imagination lucklessly de-
prived of a creative outlet.

And yet, its thematic variety notwithstanding, *Interiors'* first
half (like Eve herself) is so sedulously observant of detail that
it fairly cries out for contrast. And almost precisely at narrative

mid-point, when Renata hosts a dinner for the returning Arthur, that contrast arrives in the hip-swaying, red-dress-billow-
ing presence of Pearl (Maureen Stapleton)—like Miles in
Sleeper's futureworld, the "alien" come to energize and
threaten a homogenous society. Also as with Miles, Pearl's
alienation has the double-edged effect of challenging and coa-
lescing the existing forces. What are differences between Eve,
Renata, and Joey in light of this garish affront to their femininity and shared past? Despite (and, one senses, also because of)
Arthur's pleas for tolerance, Pearl's entrance thrusts the hitherto impartial Joey into loyal alliance with her mother; while
Eve, upon sensing competition, turns from restrained interior
decorating to flamboyant Catholicism, from domestic to mystical ritual, in an increasingly deranged search for formulas.

During her early scenes, Pearl is patently the family's foil.
Effusive where they're inhibited, earthily, almost slovenly physical while they're intellectual, she's the Knicks game to their
Dysentery discussions. When she's seen one cathedral, she's
seen them all; the closest she's likely to come to high culture
is her son's "art gallery" in Caesar's Palace in Las Vegas; and
after the various family members offer predictably tortuous,
self-oriented observations of an off-Broadway play, Pearl comments, "I didn't see that. To me the one guy was a squealer, the
other wasn't. I liked the guy who wasn't a squealer." Where
Renata and Frederich competitively bicker, where Joey can't
accept Mike's devotion, Pearl and Arthur are glowingly, in-
dulgingly happy with one another. And while Joey finds Pearl
unequivocally a "vulgarian," our response is more like Alvy's
"If life were only like this . . ." reaction to Marshall MacLuhan's fantasy appearance.

Still, to a mature Allen's credit, Pearl does not arrive bearing Miles's obvious social and moral solutions; finally, she is
here to complicate themes and relationships. And while she
performs her symbolic function, she also develops as an increasingly unpredictable human being. Although probably
Jewish and certainly a mother, she bears no resemblance to
masked Mrs. Starkwell or illness-obsessed Mrs. Singer, or to
the upcoming Mrs. Bates, whose chief activity will consist of
"putting the chicken through the deflavorizing machine." In

contrast to all Allen has told us about Jews, and especially about Jewish mothers, Pearl has fun. With two unmourned husbands in her past, she travels widely and indiscriminately, enjoys the beach, card tricks, reading palms and is prone to bursts of common sense, such as, "You'll live to be a hundred if you give up all the things that make you want to." Yet, in Maureen Stapleton's sensitive portrayal there's a restiveness to Pearl's ebullience, a vulnerability implied in her joyous attempts to make peace with Arthur's family, and her face often looks perplexed, almost sorrowful in repose. The anxious Renatas and Eves and Joeys of the world are not an elite class: life is a mystery to Pearl as well.

It's a mark of Allen's growth that he can now scrutinize his "alien" both from without and within. Pearl's flamboyant red dress is not inherently lovelier, only different from Eve's beiges and whites. The very characteristic which most attracts Arthur to Pearl—her affectionate indifference to ideals, personal or aesthetic—is merely the reverse of Eve's once-seductive perfectionism. Thus *Interiors* again evokes *Love and Death*'s two half-wrongs in a social and aesthetic context. And like Boris's, our inclinations vacillate: Pearl's conviviality is a relief after Eve's rigidity; but then Pearl's haphazard, day-to-day living offsets Eve's albeit misdirected search for standards and transcendent truths as courageous. And our allegiances are equally with both women when Pearl casually and unfeelingly suggests brightening up Eve's pale decorations, and when, carried away by her own high spirits, Pearl dances into Eve's vase and sends it shattering to the floor.

The two half-wrongs of Eve and Pearl are most compellingly pursued in a scene in St. Patrick's Cathedral, where the troubled Arthur comes to tell Eve of his new attachment. As in all *Interiors'* finest moments, the setting is symbolic, but the feelings conveyed are delicate and believably human. In one shot, the camera dwells on Arthur sadly observing the nervously chattering Eve, as if he were perceiving a bruised artifact from a cherished past. And when Eve strikes the row of red candles, she is symbolically attacking Pearl (with her red dress) and denying Catholic faith; but she is also literally venting credible frustration on the nearest object.

In sharp contrast to *Manhattan, Interiors* is most involving
when it confronts bold conflicts—between Eve and Pearl, past
and present, art and life—and least effective when describing
social rituals. The wedding and funeral are both without distinguishing details, and Frederich's inebriated flirtations with
Flynn, herself barely credible as a family member, merely clut-
ter the narrative. On the other hand, Joey's faithful boyfriend
Mike might have been more fully developed, as his role in
Interiors' stunning final scenes is pivotal.

And while *Interiors'* many clumped short sequences have
correlatives in the comedies, its sustained climax is a crucial
contribution to Allen's work. Operating in a shady area between myth and reality, this scene recalls both *King Lear* and
Cries and Whispers. Yet, where Shakespeare and Bergman concentrate on a dying protagonist's getting of wisdom, Allen
stresses the survivor's getting of psychic liberation.

Situated after the wedding party, the scene opens as most of
the family members retire to their bedrooms and Joey, unable
to sleep, wanders outside and discovers her mother:

> Mother, is that you? You shouldn't be here, not
> tonight . . . It's ironic because I care for you so; and
> you have nothing but disdain for me. And yet, I feel
> guilty . . . I think you're really too perfect for this
> world . . . Oh, mother, don't you see? You're not just
> a sick woman. That would be too easy. The truth is
> there's been perverseness and willfulness of attitude
> in many of the things you've done.

Since Joey is cathartically musing to herself, Eve is fittingly
obscured in shadow. And the scene proceeds in half-light as
Joey quietly confesses, "But I love you," as Eve rushes toward
the sea, and Pearl follows Joey from house to ocean. Inside,
Arthur, Renata, Frederich, and Flynn gently sleep. And the
camera periodically returns to them, as Mike rushes past Pearl
to struggle with and finally wrench a collapsed Joey from the
waves which have swallowed her mother; as Pearl bends in
earthy assurance to artificially resuscitate her stepdaughter
back to choking life. The symbolism is unmistakable here: with

egoistic, restrained Eve engulfed by a fathomless subconscious; with Mike sundering the umbilical cord between destructive mother and daughter; with Pearl giving Joey a figurative rebirth. As Allen describes this action, "In Europe they call mouth-to-mouth resuscitation the kiss of life, and that's what I wanted to convey—I wanted Pearl to breathe life into Joey."

And yet to Allen's credit, and for the first time in his work, true dramatic suspense is also evoked. Will Joey live or won't she? It matters. And while Joey's salvation is paramount, Allen simultaneously glimpses many conflicting realities. Eve plunges to her death while her ex-husband and offspring obliviously sleep. When Joey cries, "Mother!" to Eve, it is Pearl who hears and responds. While Eve selects suicide over imperfect life, Joey has survival thrust upon her.

Significantly, where Allen's earlier comedies (and, to a lesser extent, *Annie Hall* as well) force the illusion of perfect love and art to "contend with" absurd alternatives—Luna's poetry, political panaceas, marriage to a herring merchant—*Interiors'* options are less egregiously differentiated. Illusion brings little joy in this film: believing Eve to be the "perfect woman," Arthur finds himself trapped in an "ice castle" marriage. Accepting her mother's standards of artistic excellence, Joey is continually dissatisfied with her efforts, artistic and otherwise. For Joey, *Interiors'* most important characters are Mike and Pearl. And in a final scene, as she writes in a diary, Joey seems to have taken a step toward reconciliation with them, her past, and even her artistic illusions. Recognizing that she hasn't sufficient talent to perform artistically for others, she's reaping less glamorous satisfaction from confessing to a diary. "I felt compelled to write these thoughts down," she says in voice-over. "They seemed very powerful to me." And the thematic emphasis is on the *me*. Thus, for the first time, Allen champions a protagonist who eschews romantic illusions in favor of realistic compromise, preparing the way for both *Stardust Memories* and *The Floating Lightbulb*.

Like Vivian Gornick's highly subjective response to Woody's sex jokes ten years earlier, the mixed and often heatedly negative reviews of *Interiors* attest to the intimate relationship Allen has forged with his public. More in sorrow than in the anger which will greet *Stardust Memories,* sympathetic critics expressed feelings of betrayal. James Monaco, for instance, commented, "We have depended on Allen for more than ten years now as champion against just this particular sort of bad-faith artiness and the mid-cult sensibility from which it stems." Others suggested that Allen's serious observations could and should accommodate humor, and on this point Allen's own ideas are telling:

> One of the criticisms of *Interiors* was that all serious works that are worth anything have humor in them as well: they're leavened by wit. But that's simply not true. Bergman's *Persona* is a truly great film, and there's not a comic moment in it. So this was, I thought, a clichéd phrase which sounded meaningful, but in fact wasn't.

Manhattan

The Sunday before *Manhattan*'s opening, Allen reiterated his serious concerns and goals in a *New York Times* cover story, telling interviewer Natalie Gittelson, "Until we find a resolution for our terrors, we're going to have an expedient culture"; and that he was steadily "trying to advance in the direction of films that are more human and less cartoon," that "Tragedy . . . is a form to which I would ultimately like to aspire." These sobering remarks, and memories of *Interiors,* at once undermine and offset *Manhattan*'s first luminous black-and-white images (which, fittingly, are not black and white, but Gordon Willis's subtle mixture of grays), buoyantly accompanied by Gershwin's "Rhapsody in Blue." The glistening montage shots of Isaac Davis's Manhattan (with cuts from the Empire State Building, to vegetable stands, to an embracing couple high above Central Park fireworks, etc.) are exhilarating, as is the voice of this would-be autobiographical novelist: "He adored New York City. He idealized it all out of proportion—no, make that *romanticized* it all out of proportion." And yet, as when stand-up comic Woody announced, "I moved into a doorman apartment on Park Avenue," we now less gleefully await Allen's incongruity.

Beyond its conflicting dramatic undercurrents, *Manhattan*'s virtuoso opening passage assures audiences that, whatever his formal preferences, Allen is masterfully in control of the comic craft. While its ebullience immediately differentiates *Manhattan* from the preceding *Interiors,* there are significant developments since *Annie Hall* as well: Isaac Davis's religious and family affiliations are never mentioned and are thus, we presume, irrelevant; subplots which only perfunctorily involve the persona are now explored; and the classless, eclectic world of Alvy Singer has made way for a fluidly observed upper-class milieu, reminiscent of the "high comedy" settings of George Cukor's *Philadelphia Story* and Ernst Lubitsch's *Trouble in Paradise.* That Allen now dares portray the romantic hero in such a world marks a new, earned confidence in his acting range. No longer relying on Fielding's self-parodic boasts and false humility, or even Alvy's emphatic New York Jewishness, Allen's acting has never been more subtly varied. Particularly in his final scene with Tracy, he discovers resources of expression no earlier performance anticipates.

Although it gained no awards, *Manhattan* was Allen's greatest *succes d'estime,* winning glowing reviews from all quarters. Andrew Sarris, never a prominent defender, hailed it as "the only truly great film of the '70s," while the more consistently admiring Vincent Canby perceptively commented that "what happens is not the substance of *Manhattan* as much as how it happens." And insofar as *Manhattan* concentrates on "how," rather than "what" or "why," it is a nearly faultless tour de force collision between the conventions of comedy and serious ideas. With the crucial difference that moralist Isaac Davis is present, *Manhattan* recalls the life-goes-on-so-change-partners-and-dance cynicism of Schnitzler's *La Ronde,* and its plot transfers *Love and Death*'s report on the romantic climate of nineteenth-century Russia to contemporary New York. Where *Love and Death*'s counts and countesses fight duels and wars, write idle verse, and misbehave at the St. Petersburg Opera and during piano instruction, *Manhattan*'s art-dabbling New Yorkers congregate at Elaine's or Museum of Modern Art parties, publish explicit reports on their bad marriages, and arrange clandestine lunch hours in Bloomingdale's. The discrepancy, which finally proves crucial, is that while "at my back," Boris and Sonia hear Napoleon as well as "love fades," Isaac, Yale, Mary, and Tracy hear only the loss of romantic innocence.

And *Manhattan's* romantic entanglements are slightly more intricate than *Love and Death's*. College professor Yale (Michael Murphy) and comic television writer, would-be novelist Isaac (Woody) are best friends. Yale is happily married to Emily (Anne Byrne), but also adulterously in love with the neurotic divorcée journalist Mary (Diane Keaton). And though Isaac is fond of seventeen-year-old Tracy (Mariel Hemingway), who deeply loves him, he can't take her "seriously" because she's "too young." Isaac is also attracted to Mary but won't court her because she's involved with his best friend.

During the course of the film, Yale breaks up with Mary to preserve his marriage, Isaac breaks with Tracy to pursue Mary, and Mary and Isaac live together for a while. Then, Mary and Yale fall back in love so Mary leaves Isaac for Yale, Yale leaves Emily for Mary, and Isaac recongnizes Tracy's virtues perhaps too late and tries to get her back. Upon Isaac's earlier suggestion, Tracy has decided to spend six months studying acting in London; thus, in a more pessimistic variation on *Bananas,* maybe they'll get back together in six months, but probably they won't.

Allen's metaphorical "Manhattan," where the reality of an aesthetically and morally diverse modern city must "contend with" Isaac's selective romantic impressions, is echoed stylistically, in Gershwin tunes and seductive visual romanticism and narratively in characters whose attraction for Isaac is difficult to defend in terms of real qualities. It is quickly apparent that Yale, for instance, is not the energetic intellectual and devoted friend and husband Isaac supposes, but a feckless, if often charming, narcissistic man whose perennial vaguely pained expression is equally the mark of important and trivial indecision. He expends as much emotional energy deciding whether to buy the Porsche sports car as in contemplating the pros and cons of leaving his wife of fifteen years for his new lover, Mary. And Isaac is similarly unsuspecting of fundamental, if comically evoked, flaws in Mary. Though she describes herself as "trouble," Isaac is confident that he'll "be the one to change" her from an insecure ("I'm just from Philadelphia—I mean, we believe in God, O.K.?'") woman, so obsessively intellectual she's memorized the circles of Saturn, into the stable companion he now self-deceptively believes he wants to live with.

Isaac's inability to perceive his own shortcomings reflects Allen's increasingly distanced perspective on a now less lovable persona. On the one hand—and more in keeping with the tragic than the comic hero—Isaac is the most self-assured and socially prominent of Woody's descendants: he lives graciously, commands and then virtuously rejects a large salary, and offhandedly remarks that he's never had trouble meeting women. Where Miles defended his jokes as "a defense mechanism," Isaac's response to Mary's "You know, you've got a good sense of humor, you actually do," is a wry, "Hey, thanks, I don't need you to tell me that, you know. I've been making good money off it for years."

Yet Isaac is a good deal less appealing than Alvy Singer: it is not by chance that Isaac is, in his words, "winner of the August Strindberg Award" when "it comes to relationships with women." Far more than Alvy, he's obviously stimulated by "trouble." He married his first wife Jill (Meryl Streep) realizing that she was bisexual. And during the course of *Manhattan* he's drawn first to Mary, with her attachments to Yale and log of problematic relationships, and then to the generous Tracy only when it's conveniently too late. Though he emerges as the most upstanding of a slothful, irresolute adult community, Issac has moral drawbacks of his own: Jill's account of the "disgusting little moments" of their married life, including the time when he tried to run over her female lover, turn out to be true. And often his valiant gestures are impulsive. After quitting his well-paid television job, he feels like a hero "for about thirty seconds, and then it's directly to unemployment."

Just as *Interiors* reduces the discrepancy between illusion and reality, *Manhattan* blurs the line between protagonist and satirical victim. Where the earlier comedies comfortably discover their targets *out there*—in a futureworld Orb or a herring merchant or *Annie Hall*'s California—*Manhattan* more disconcertingly parodies its main characters. The *Getting Even* prototype is no longer a pontificating Columbia professor but professor Yale and especially Mary, who, when we first meet her, is self-aggrandizingly abrading a photography exhibit at the Whitney Museum: "I really felt it was very derivative. To me, it was straight out of Diane Arbus, but it had none of the wit." And Mary and Yale have invented an "Academy of the Overrated" which includes such artistic unworthies as Norman Mailer, Lenny Bruce, Gustav Mahler, Van Gogh—pronounced Go*k*—and Ingmar Bergman: yet these two pretentious intellectuals are Isaac's friends and lovers. And where Alvy Singer had to travel to Los Angeles to excoriate banal television humor, Isaac, at the start of *Manhattan*, is himself employed by a television show called "Human Beings, Wow," which transforms his writing into material which is "antiseptic," "empty," and "worse than not insightful—it's not funny."

Like Pearl in *Interiors*, awkwardly beautiful, seventeen-year-old Tracy stands in lonely opposition to *Manhattan*'s homogeneous and now degenerate community. Observed out of context, the "great sex" she has with Isaac and such infinitely wise remarks as "Maybe people aren't meant to have one deep relationship—maybe we're meant to have, you know, a series of relationships of different lengths," a bit too conveniently foil the convoluted physical and intellectual relations of the others. Yet, with her long, soft face resting on Allen's craggy shoulder, Hemingway is a visually appealing incongruous mate; and like Maureen Stapleton, she brings a sorrowful unpredictability to her character. And Tracy is not always the wise youth. In one of *Manhattan*'s loveliest scenes she's childishly requested an old-fashioned carriage ride through Central Park. As she thoroughly enjoys herself, Isaac fittingly remarks, "You're God's answer to Job . . . 'I do a lot of terrible things, but I can also make one of these.' "

Cinematically, *Manhattan* is at once Allen's lushest and most economical work. Where *Annie Hall* employs images, dialogue, and subtitles to convey Alvy and Annie's courtship, *Manhattan* creates a similar tension between romantic excitement and irony, particular and general experience, through its images and soundtrack tunes alone. The four pivotal scenes which evoke Isaac and Mary's romance are indicative. In a first, sustained image, which might be labelled "Initial Attraction," Isaac and Mary are portrayed as two distant gray cartoon

silhouettes, watching dawn rise over the Fifty-ninth Street
Bridge to the plaintive strains of "Someone to Watch Over
Me." And, intercut among more realistically observed action,
the courtship images continue: with a shot of Mary and Isaac's
blurry features flirting in a glass museum display bowl; in a
montage of lovers' activities in the city and then, to the tune of
" 'S'Wonderful," in shots of a day in the country.

In self-parodic contrast to *Annie Hall, Manhattan* places the
Allen character in the role of tempering Keaton's now avid
cerebral interests with comments like, "The brain is the most
overrated organ, I think . . . Everything really valuable has to
enter you through a different opening, if you'll forgive the
disgusting imagery." And in keeping with the half-truth of this
statement, *Manhattan* deftly pursues the mind/body conflict,
often by juxtaposing image and word. The appealing visual
naiveté of a soda fountain scene, for instance, is contrasted with
its disconcerting dialogue, in which Isaac explains that he's
leaving Tracy for another woman.

And a sequence where Emily reads aloud from Jill's recently
published diatribe against ex-husband Isaac collides image and
word, narcissism and intelligent self-awareness with breathtak-
ing subtlety. As the scene begins, Emily reads, " 'He had complaints about life, but no solutions . . . .' " while the camera
focuses on a gloomy Isaac. Here the opposition is intelligent,
but its point is straightforward: Jill's harsh verbal accusations
are valid, and so is the visual fact of Isaac's misery. But now
Allen insidiously complicates his mise-en-scene. For as Emily
continues reading, "In his most private moments, he spoke of
a fear of death, which he elevated to tragic heights, when in fact
it was mere narcissism," Isaac suddenly vanishes from the
frame—thus his fears of death are cinematically justified. And
this idea is more stridently reiterated in a later scene in which
Isaac lectures Yale on moral priorities while absurdly posi-
tioned in front of a classroom skeleton. When Yale demands,
"Where are you going?" Isaac vanishes from the scene, leaving
the skeleton alone in the frame. Manifestly, *there* is where he
is, and we all are, ultimately going.

Although the scenes between Isaac and Yale, Mary, or Tracy
are Allen's surest, subplot sequences between Mary and Yale

—during a Bloomingdale's lunch hour, breaking up over a civilized cocktail at the Stanhope Café—stretch refreshingly beyond autobiographical material; as do two not entirely convincing, and yet touching, scenes between Isaac and his small son, first at the Russian Tea Room and later emerging from a "Divorced Fathers" Sunday football game. By casting Keaton as a woman who describes herself as "beautiful" and "brainy," whose analyst calls *her* to cry in the middle of the night, and who won't discuss what she'll be doing in a month because, "I can't plan that far in advance," Allen coolly plays against the zany lovableness of Annie Hall. And also atypical—and intriguing—is the fact that *Manhattan* turns to a bisexual ex-wife rather than a Brooklyn childhood for expository information on its protagonist.

Manhattan introduces two sometimes overlapping moral conflicts. The first, as in *Interiors,* is the challenge of exhibiting moral courage in a society which rewards more glamorous virtues; and the second is a tension between youth's relatively simple and maturity's more complex vision of moral options: in other words, will Tracy maintain her purity of spirit when she experiences more complicated emotions and opportunities?

To leave this latter, sensitively developed conflict for a moment, it is when approaching the "why" of Yale's want of moral courage, in a classroom confrontation between Isaac and his best friend, that *Manhattan* briefly loses its balance between comic tone and serious idea. The confrontation evolves when Isaac learns that Yale has been clandestinely meeting Mary and that the two are now planning to live together. Unable to contend with Mary ("I can't express anger . . . I get an ulcer instead"), Isaac literally pulls Yale from his lecture hall into an adjacent classroom, accusing:

> You rationalize everything . . . You talk about you
> want to write a book, but in the end you'd rather buy
> the Porsche . . . You cheat a little on Emily, and you
> play around with the truth a little with me, and the
> next thing you know, you're in front of a Senate
> Sub-Committee, and you're naming names.

As the camera holds Isaac's small, angry head in tight close-up with the motionless, grimacing skull of a classroom skeleton, the moralist continues:

> What are future generations gonna say about us?
> . . . Some day we're gonna be like him . . . He was
> probably one of the beautiful people . . . It's very
> important to have some kind of integrity . . . I'll be
> hanging in a classroom one day, and I want to
> make sure that when I thin out that I'll be well
> thought of.

Despite visual complexities, and intricate allusions—notably to *The Front* and Hamlet's musings over the corpse of his dead tutor, Yorick—this scene is dramatically overbearing beyond its narrative and thematic impact. In contrast to Boris's debated assassination of Napoleon, there's no moral tension, since Yale is obviously in the wrong. But more important in light of Allen's dramatic ambitions, this scene imposes tragic expectations of "integrity" and "truth" on a comically delineated character. Up to this point the convention of comic absurdity has effectively "disconnected" pleasant comic prototypes Yale and Mary from their symbolic perfidies. Mary's bizarre dialogue (for instance, "My problem is that I'm both attracted and repelled by the male organ"), Yale's parodied vacillations, even Isaac's skulduggery (his attempt to run over his wife's lover): these comic exaggerations permit Allen to condemn the deed while affectionately exonerating the doer. But now, as he attempts to segue into the conventions of tragedy, Allen asks that we seriously judge character and predilection as an organic whole; and this is a demand and a journey he has not yet earned.

Manhattan's other moral dilemma is more persuasively pursued in Isaac's shamefaced return to the now inaccessible Tracy. At once parodying and poignantly reevoking a history of movie "coups de foudre," this scene opens with a disgruntled Isaac reclining, like Professor Higgins, on his couch, asking and responding to "Why is life worth living?":

> Groucho Marx, Willie Mays, the Second Movement of the Jupiter Symphony, Louis Armstrong's recording of "Potato Head Blues" . . . Tracy's face . . .

As with Gaston in *Gigi,* the thunderbolt of romantic truth strikes Isaac, who suddenly realizes that Tracy is indeed the "perfect woman." And to a medley of Gershwin tunes, Isaac traverses New York's most gleamingly romantic streets, from his door to Tracy's, finally glimpsing from afar the image of this wholesome young woman mysteriously brushing her hair like a Rembrandt bather. With the yearning and self-effacement of Chaplin approaching the no-longer-blind girl at the end of *City Lights,* Isaac gingerly proceeds toward the woman he has mistakenly rejected. But, as the soundtrack confirms with "They're Playing Songs of Love, But Not for Me," Tracy is scheduled to leave for London at any moment. "What's six months, if we still love each other?" she reasonably demands of an anxious Isaac. "You'll change," he insists. And as Tracy replies, "Everybody gets corrupted . . . have a little faith in people," Isaac's half-smile conveys precisely the mixture of disbelief and unfounded hope evoked by Chaplin under *City Lights'* very different circumstances.

In sharp contrast both to *Interiors* and to such "high comedy" classics as *Philadelphia Story, Trouble in Paradise* and *Design for Living, Manhattan* ends, not with romantic compromise or with corruption finding and liking its own, but with Isaac still hoping for something far better than he deserves.

=8=

Full Circle

Side Effects,   Stardust Memories,
The Floating Lightbulb

There's a fantasy sequence in *Stardust Memories* that is echoed in the *Side Effects* story "The Lunatic's Tale." In each case, a man falls in love with a seemingly "perfect woman" who soon ceases to attract him sexually; at which point he develops an inconvenient sexual yen for a woman who otherwise disgusts him. Being a gifted surgeon, the man operates to correct his painfully incongruous love impulses, transferring the lovable traits into the voluptuous body and the unbecoming personal qualities into the less arousing body. Miraculously, the operation is totally successful, but soon the man is passionately in pursuit of yet another woman he despises.

"I think that as you get older your vision gets darker," comments Allen, and these acrid cautionary tales suggest a dark passage in Allen's art, confirmed throughout the four strongest *Side Effects* stories, *Stardust Memories,* and *The Floating Lightbulb.* The luck which defined talent for Isaac Davis is now a slippery, fickle quality, alarmingly like Greek fate, which adumbrates an increasingly wide range of human experience. Imagination, talent, fame are no armor against its whims, and, as in "Death," since luck's ways are inscrutable there's no logical course of ingratiation, no "plan." And lucklessness is a good deceiver, often assuming the guise of good fortune. Were

Sandy Bates and the doctor narrator lucky or unlucky to meet "perfect" mates, and were their miraculous operations successful or quite the opposite? Is stuttering closet magician Paul lucky, as his mother suggests, to be visited by a New York agent? And what of Sandy Bates's lucid vision of parallel trains, the one bearing the beautiful, the other the grotesques of the earth? Like "heaven and angels and saints" versus "people cashing in," like naming names versus telling HUAC "You can fuck yourselves," the options appear so satisfyingly clear-cut. And yet both trains travel to the same remote, desolate junkyard.

Allen has indeed come full circle. Though the early Woody was a singularly unlucky fellow—assaulted by doormen, expelled from college, persecuted by machines and the Ku Klux Klan—he had the luck to be moving within a comically perceived world. There was always the possibility of happy deliverance—the Ku Klux Klan might be moved by his eloquence; Nancy might, in a moment of romantic insanity, marry him; he could always whittle a soap gun and hope to again escape from jail. But life is not so straightforward for the now objectively lucky Sandy Bates, or for most of the *Side Effects* characters. Alvy Singer couldn't do his homework because the universe was everything, and the universe was shrinking. Now the universe has shrunk, and jail is not punishment for robbing a bank but the human condition, relieved only by death, a trip to the junkyard which is, in the words of Boris, "even worse than the food at Kresge's."

"When I was younger I used to get more of a personal kick out of just being funny," says Allen, and so did his earlier prototypes. Confronted with the unconfortably conspicuous position of being a "real Jew" at the Halls' Easter table, Alvy Singer finds fantasy release in a comic juxtaposition of Annie's family and his own. But magician Paul isn't funny and, except as a ploy to seduce desirable women, Sandy Bates has no use for humor. Though he can produce it on automatic pilot, comedy is boring and meaningless for him. And, not coincidentally, the best of the *Side Effects* stories exploit a black, rueful humor rather than the exuberant broad, parodic comedy of *Getting Even* and *Without Feathers*. When essays such as "The UFO

Menace" or "Remembering Needleman" strive to reevoke the
Perelmanesque glee of "The Metterling Lists" and "Viva Vargas," they feel forced and listless; clearly Allen's ambitions are
no longer here.

Where *Interiors* diminishes the discrepancy between fantasy
and reality, *Stardust Memories, The Floating Lightbulb,* and
Side Effects go further, sometimes to vitiate, sometimes to question the efficacy of fantasy release. Where the cinematic "vanishing" of Isaac, as Emily reads Jill's literary complaints against
his narcissism, subtly intimates his inevitable death; Sandy
Bates's many imagined "vanishings" and Enid's observation,
"I'd like to vanish," clearly spell out death wishes. And while
fantasy brought Fielding release from revolution and Boris
from the Napoleonic wars, the daydream and romantic escapes
of Allen's later characters are often no more prepossessing than
real life. In "The Kugelmass Episode," Kugelmass wearily discovers that a demanding "fantasy" Emma Bovary at the Plaza
is no more romantic than a demanding "real" wife and a boring
job. And Sandy Bates's surgical fantasy of creating and falling
out of love with the "perfect woman" is only the metaphorical
story of his life at present.

And if fantasy in these recent works is often no more satisfying than real life, magic is often disconcertingly like real work.
Paul labors to create his magic effects, and after "The Great
Sandy" has performed a seemingly effortless feat, his mother
announces that he practices six hours a day. The making of
Sandy Bates's buoyant comic films is similarly an arduous matter of quarrelling with producers, tussling with fans, and enduring energy-consuming doubts about the ultimate validity of it
all.

With *The Floating Lightbulb* as exception, these works are
preoccupied with a conflict between body and mind in which
a luckless mixture of external fate and a character's own irrational impulses dooms a nonetheless dogged search for the
"perfect woman." As with his victimization, there was an implied optimism to the sexual thwarting of the earlier persona,
for almost always he was object rather than perpetrator of
romantic unreasonableness. Nancy found "something missing"
in him, Annie stopped wanting sex, Mary left him for his best

friend. And yet, exterior problems notwithstanding, Woody
was quite romantically reasonable. "If life were only like
this . . . ," sighs Alvy Singer of his MacLuhan fantasy—and
wasn't it pretty to think so, to believe that if life, and especially
romance, were as Woody would have it, all would be well.

But *Stardust Memories* and essays such as "The Lunatic's
Tale" present a less comfortable and, one senses, more artistically honest point of view. Far from a romantic underdog, the
more recent Allen prototype has little trouble winning the love
of desirable women. Long-nosed would-be-playwright Harold
Cohen of "Retribution" is immediately attractive to beautiful,
intelligent, Connecticut-born Connie Chasen, and Sandy Bates
effortlessly seduces every woman he wants in *Stardust Memories.* Yet Sandy, Harold, and the "lunatic" doctor also lose their
women, and not only because the women are sexually unpredictable, but because of their own sexual unreasonableness and,
beyond this, because of the ultimate unreasonableness of life. In
a Freudian variation on Donne's "Song," finding and keeping
the woman "true and fair" is a "Go and catch a falling star"
proposition; still, Allen's characters are wearily stretching out
their arms.

Side Effects

As with *Interiors* as opposed to *Annie Hall,* the four strongest *Side Effects* stories are written in straightforward, often
consciously measured prose, and, but for bursts of Jewish
humor, are less distinctly Allen's than "The Metterling Lists"
or "The Whore of Mensa." Now description rather than parodic style distances author from characters, who are more like
the protagonists in the films and plays than the *Getting Even*
and *Without Feathers* narrators; and, as in the nightclub acts,
seemingly direct presentation often obscures thematic clues and
complex ideas.

In "The Shallowest Man," for instance, a group of poker
friends sit around a delicatessen table, casually reappraising the
story of fellow poker players Mendel—in one man's opinion,
"positively the shallowest human" he's ever known—and the
now deceased Meyer Iskowitz. Though excessively discomfited

by thoughts of death and the atmosphere of hospital rooms
(" . . . Suffocating. And the lunch trays and the bedpans and
elderly and lame . . ."), Mendel regularly visited his dying
acquaintance Meyer Iskowitz for the sole purpose of courting
Meyer's beautiful nurse, Miss Hill. Unaware of Mendel's ulte-
rior motives, Meyer was embarrassingly grateful for Mendel's
attentions. One of the men concludes the story:

> On a rainy April day Iskowitz died. Before expiring
> he told Mendel once again that he loved him and
> that Mendel's concern for him in these last months
> was the most touching and deepest experience he
> ever had with a human being. Two weeks later Miss
> Hill . . . and Mendel started dating . . . They had an
> affair that lasted a year and then they went their
> separate ways.

And, in *Rashomon* fashion, the other poker friends bring various interpretations to the tale. "It goes to show how some
people are just no damn good," insists one. Another muses,
"The story shows how the love of a woman enables a man to
overcome his fears of mortality if only for a while." A third and
fourth observe:

> What's the difference? . . . Iskowitz experienced a
> closeness. He died comforted. That it was motivated
> by Mendel's lust for the nurse—so?

And:

> Lust? Who said lust? Mendel, despite his shal-
> lowness, may have felt love for the first time in his
> life.

A final voice, like Sonia's after the herring merchant's death in
Love and Death, has heard enough of morality: "Who cares
what the point of the story is? . . . It was an entertaining
anecdote. Let's order."

As will be true with Sandy Bates in *Stardust Memories,*
Allen deftly juggles our feelings toward Mendel: on the one

hand, we are encouraged to guiltily share his aversion to hospitals; on the other, Mendel's self-coddling indifference and then self-indulging attentions to the suffering Meyer Iskowitz are intentionally off-putting; so he's too idiosyncratic to serve as Everyman. And, in contrast to *Rashomon,* although there's a bit of truth to each poker player's analysis, more stimulating questions are left unobserved: was Miss Hill objectively very beautiful, or was Mendel's perception skewed by the mortality her good health contrasted with? Was Mendel finally punished—by the dissolution of his affair—for his duplicity in respect to Meyer?

Again as in the club routines, "The Shallowest Man" conveys a good deal of seemingly extraneous information. Two of its twelve pages, for instance, concentrate on Mendel's antipathy to the appurtenances of death, in observations like:

> He was not religious and not a hero and not a stoic,
> and during the course of his day-to-day existence he
> didn't want to know from funerals or hospitals or
> terminal wards. If a hearse went by in the street the
> image might stay with him for hours . . . And what
> if all the speculation of cancer is true? I should be
> in the same room as Meyer Iskowitz? Who knows if
> it's catching?

Yet far from arbitrary, this surfeit of hypochondriacal data presents a case for Mendel's not visiting Meyer even once, which renders his decision to return nightly quite extraordinary. Lust, or love, must be intense indeed if it overpowers so insistent an aversion; and taking this point the intended step further, how inexorable then are the powers of "love fades" if they can quench a passion as fervent as Mendel's. The seemingly superfluous presences of the poker players are also thematically salient. Beyond suggesting many possible readings of even a "shallow" man's behavior, these men—like the soldier in *Love and Death*'s "little hygiene play" sequence—attest to the futility of the cautionary tale, real or apochryphal. In art as in life, one perceives what one wants to perceive.

Introducing narrators more endearingly akin to the persona

than to Mendel, "The Lunatic's Tale" and "Retribution" bring a human dimension to the irrationality of love. At the start of "The Lunatic's Tale," its famous doctor narrator is, in his words, "on the surface apparently blessed with all the necessities for the good life. Underneath, desperately in search of a fulfilling love." And assuming the tone of Allan Felix, would-be playwright Harold Cohen opens "Retribution" commenting: "That Connie Chasen returned my fatal attraction toward her at first sight was a miracle unparalleled in the history of Central Park West."

Like the poker players, the "lunatic" and Harold Cohen acknowledge different priorities under thematically similar circumstances. As previously noted, "The Lunatic's Tale" throws up its figurative arms at the impotence of science and logic before the irrational impulses of the body. Sorrowfully, the doctor allows sexual predilection to lead him from the "perfect woman" to a mindless stewardess and finally to madness. "Retribution" 's Harold Cohen, on the other hand, follows his mind and a seemingly wiser, safer course of action. When he falls in love with his lover Connie Chasen's mother, Emily, Harold sublimates his desires in filial attentions. Proud of his restraint, Harold returns home to Connie a stronger and more committed man. What is his reward? Connie is no longer the sexually voracious mate she was: though consciously happy that Harold and her mother have established a rapport, subconsciously Connie now equates Harold with her brother. Unwilling and then unable to sleep with Harold, Connie finally, sadly ends their relationship; and shortly thereafter Emily Chasen and her husband divorce. Though still in love with Connie, Harold marries Emily because "I couldn't swing it with the daughter, so I carried off the mother." On his wedding day, Harold is approached by a now insatiably attracted Connie: "It's a whole new ball game," she explains. ". . . Marrying Mom has made you my father."

While explicitly scrambling Freud's, Sophocles', and O'Neill's versions of the Electra myth, "Retribution" takes a light-hearted approach to the lover's damned-if-you-do-damned-if-you-don't conflict between conscience and desire. As Sandy Bates will observe in *Stardust Memories,* "I think any relationship isn't based on compromise or maturity or perfection, or any of that—it's really based on luck. People don't like to acknowledge that because it means a lack of control."

For all its broadly comic clues (Connie's family name "Chasen," the "fatal attraction" noted in the opening sentence), "Retribution" is among Allen's subtlest and most sympathetically etched stories. A subplot in which Harold compares his Jewish family with the Connecticut Chasens ironically reevokes Alvy Singer's Easter visit to the Halls. Though he initially marvels at the Chasens' affectionate rapport, when Emily and her husband divorce, Harold perplexedly observes, "My parents fight like the Montagues and Capulets and stay together their entire lives. Connie's folks sip martinis and hug with true civility and, bingo, they're divorcing." And when Connie displays her true Electra predilections at the end, Harold/Allen finishes with a tribute to prosaic Jewish predictability: ". . . and all I could mutter to myself as I remained a limp, hunched figure was an age-old line of my grandfather's which goes, 'Oy vey.' "

The best of these stories, "The Kugelmass Episode" (described in the Introduction), affectingly portrays the mind/body conflict as part of a larger tension between reality and fantasy. To briefly reiterate: Kugelmass, a middle-aged humanities professor and analysand, "unhappily married for a second time," wants "romance" and "music" and "love" and "beauty" in his routine existence. Impatient with the slow progress of his psychoanalysis, Kugelmass seeks out a magician called "The Great Persky," who, true to his promise, transports Kugelmass to Emma Bovary's nineteenth-century France and back to New York only a few minutes late to meet the current Mrs. Kugelmass at Bloomingdale's. But as Kugelmass persists in his clandestine magic, fantasy becomes as arduous as reality. Mrs. Kugelmass grows increasingly suspicious, Emma Bovary emboldenedly demanding, and one day Persky's magic fails, and Kugelmass is excruciatingly trapped between real life and fantasy obligations. After this chastening experience, Kugelmass forswears magic; but one fine day three weeks later, ". . . Persky answered his doorbell. It was Kuglemass, with a sheepish expression on his face."

The significant difference between "The Kugelmass Episode" and the other stories is its gentle tone and more universal application. In contrast to Mendel, the "lunatic" doctor and Harold Cohen, Kugelmass is not a conspicuously successful New Yorker, but a middle-aged man who, like Word Babcock in "The Whore of Mensa," desires beyond his romantic appeal. "I may not look the part," Kugelmass tells his psychiatrist, "but I'm a man who needs romance. I need softness. I need flirtation. I'm not getting younger, so before it's too late I want to make love in Venice, trade quips at '21,' and exchange coy glances over red wine and candlelight.'" And why shouldn't he?

More than in any of the other stories, author *and* protagonist know precisely why; and thus their most extravagant flights of fancy are dragged earthward by an almost weary wisdom. "I'm going to regret this," thinks Kugelmass as he enters the Great Persky's apartment for the first time. And Allen's careful description of Persky's shoddy "magic" equipment (a "cheap-looking Chinese cabinet," a "couple of ugly rhinestones ground into the raw plywood") stays with us, even as Kugelmass and Emma Bovary soar to romantic heights.

There's also a wistfulness to Kugelmass's self-deprecating humor. For where Harold Cohen and the "lunatic" doctor (like Alvy Singer and Isaac Davis) are flamboyantly, but unnecessarily, insecure, Kugelmass's comic self-effacements have the ring of self-awareness. Indeed, he's been in analysis so long he approaches even magic with "realistic" expectations: he is convinced, for instance, that he must "enter" *Madame Bovary* before page 120, where Emma's handsome lover Rodolphe makes his first appearance. And in a moment of ecstasy (when stand-up-comic Woody would be thinking of baseball players), Kugelmass muses:

> I've earned this . . . I've suffered long enough. I've paid enough analysts. I've searched till I'm weary. [Emma's] young and nubile, and I'm here a few pages after Leon and just before Rodolphe. By showing up during the correct chapters, I've got the situation knocked.

But of course this reasonable man hasn't got the situation "knocked" any more than Harold Cohen does. As in "Retribution," life has its interfering way with the best-intentioned of mortals. Yet, unlike Harold, Kugelmass is a simple, unprepossessing fellow, "bald and hairy as a bear." There's no aura of Fate here, and nothing so glamorous as tragedy is likely to descend upon beleaguered Kugelmass. Nonetheless, as this story insists, "he had a soul"; and though he loses faith in magic, like Alvy in *Annie Hall*, he still needs "the eggs."

Stardust Memories

At the opening of *Stardust Memories*, Sandy Bates is a few crucial steps beyond the bittersweet illusions of Kugelmass and Alvy Singer. No longer searching for eggs, he seems to be blankly staring into a yard of dead chickens. Though he's still officially functioning—defending his latest film to dissatisfied producers, confirming doctors' appointments, agreeing to be honored at a Sandy Bates film retrospective weekend at the Stardust Hotel—his "soul" is clearly elsewhere. Indeed, it may well be travelling with the soul and mind of the "lunatic" doctor who, following his disastrous, successful operation, resorts to roaming "through Central Park wearing moth-eaten clothes and a surgical mask, screaming revolutionary slogans and laughing hysterically." The salient difference is that Sandy isn't laughing. Where *Manhattan*'s glimmering opening images set up comic expectations, the opening passage of *Stardust Memories*, which is in fact a tentative ending to Sandy's latest film, is symmetrically balanced between comic and tragic realms—evidently Allen is now prepared to sacrifice superficial luster to earn the rights of the serious dramatist.

We first glimpse Sandy Bates unhappily ensconced in a train car filled with grotesque, inexplicably anguished people. There's an obese man, a disconsolately weeping man, a tall blond man with the authoritarian features of a Nazi and the emaciated body of a concentration camp victim. By far the most attractive, most normal passenger, Sandy has a perplexed expression on his face, which is almost funny—because isn't this Miles in futureworld, Boris in nineteenth-century Russia, and didn't Alvy Singer have a joke about the world being divided between the horrible and the just miserable?

Now Allen/Sandy cuts to a celebratory train on the opposite side of the tracks, where comely, laughing, jewel- and fur-bedecked passengers toast one another; and we are again inclined to laugh because isn't this the old unlucky Woody, Fielding Mellish condemned to his solitary apartment while his would-be date hosts a pornographic movie party for *friends?* As with the autobiographical allusions in *Annie Hall,* Allen at once invites and refuses to confirm analogies, now to a younger comic artist *and* persona. If Sandy would drop his lip the familiar, self-parodic quarter of an inch, we, the audience, would glean our comic release. But he won't—apparently, this new persona has gone beyond Isaac's moral outrage to a desperation which does not admit of laughter, and thus our own laughs stick in our throats. Although he looks familiar, this character is manifestly not the persona we anticipate.

Now the train is moving, and Sandy flags a conductor to protest the injustice of his condition—look, he admonishes, his ticket was for the other, happier, more glamorous train. When the indifferent conductor shrugs his shoulders, Sandy thrashes against the sealed train door, to no avail. And finally nothing is to any avail, for when his train stops at a barren junkyard, hovered over by seagulls, the beautiful people have landed here as well. Allen now stretches beyond the irony of the Groucho Marx joke—not only is life awful, and there's so little of it; but when it's over, the lovely and the grotesque, the gifted and untalented, the lucky and unlucky, all wind up mystifyingly dead together.

The very allegorical simplicity of this opening sequence gives Allen the freedom to consider both tragic and comic implications. Significantly, though he won't affirm, Allen never denies the potential humor of this scene; the fact that Alvy Singer, for instance, would find it inherently funny. And thus Allen distances himself from an "anhedonic" persona especially innured to the pleasures of comedy. In *Manhattan*'s two "vanishing" sequences (where Emily reads Jill's complaints and where Yale asks "Where are you going?"), verbal accusations are juxtaposed to Isaac's visible misery and then to his absence. Now the persona's self-accusations and self-indulgence are encapsulated in one despairing, unvanishing image. This is a powerful, discomfiting scene, and by eschewing the palliating, ingratiating smokescreen of comic tone, Allen wins the dramatic prerogative to make his audience squirm.

More honest and considerably less engaging than *Manhattan, Stardust Memories* was almost universally misunderstood by the critical community. Again, the audience's intense identification with "Woody" prompted personal and now often irate responses, which were in turn thrust back not so much at Allen the artist as at Mr. Allen the human being. "So Mr. Allen hates his fans," was a common response to Sandy Bates's brusque avoidance of the Stardust's grotesquely portrayed guests. Those aware of Allen's mutually respectful relationships with Rollins, Joffe, and United Artists wondered, "How could Mr. Allen so egregiously misinterpret his sympathetic producer/agents and distributors?" The answer is, of course, that Sandy Bates is not the *real* Woody Allen, out of the closet at last, but an imaginative creation sharing many of Allen's tendencies, but also, in Allen's words, "a very sick, neurotic almost nervous-breakdown film director. I didn't want this guy to be necessarily likable. I wanted him to be surly and upset: not a saint or an angel, but a man with real problems who finds that art doesn't save you (an idea I had explored in *Interiors*)." On the subject of the fan/celebrity relationship, Allen told me:

> So many people were outraged that I dared to suggest an ambivalent, love/hate relationship between an audience and a celebrity; and then shortly after *Stardust Memories* opened, John Lennon was shot by the very guy who had asked him for his autograph earlier in the day. I feel that obtains. The guy who asks Sandy for his autograph on the boardwalk and says, "you're my favorite comedian" in the middle of the picture, later, in Sandy's fantasy, comes up and shoots him. This is what happens with celebrities—one day people love you, the next day they want to kill you. And the celebrity also feels that way toward the audience; because in the movie Sandy hallucinates that the guy shoots him; but in

fact Sandy is the one who has the gun. So the celebrity imagines that the fan will do to him what in fact
he wants to do to the fan. But people don't want to
hear this—this is an unpleasant truth to dramatize.

Also unpleasant, and personally as well as artistically daring,
is *Stardust Memories'* examination of the misanthropic inclinations of a famous man. For to cajole the self-preoccupation and
skulduggery of a social loser—to have an oblivious Allan Felix
push a man off the Golden Gate Bridge, to have Fielding Mellish gleefully precipitate a car crash—is comic convention. But
to observe similar tendencies in a social winner—to have Sandy
Bates swat away his admirers like flies and reject beautiful
women—is more like a comic death wish. And indeed, in keeping with its protagonist's state of mind, the comic death wish
is one of many things *Stardust Memories* is about. "Life is a
comedy for those who think, a tragedy for those who feel,"
wrote Walpole, and Sandy Bates is a naturally funny man who
is increasingly unable to take a thoughtful (i.e., comic) attitude
toward what feels like tragedy. This latest persona pushes
Allen's lofty versus pragmatic incongruity to an excruciating,
but also logical, extreme. Pragmatically, Sandy Bates realizes
that he should heed the advice of the "super-intelligent beings"
who warn him, "Make funnier films." But in his lofty, self-
coddling soul, Sandy no longer believes that comic filmmaking
is worthwhile. And in contrast to Alvy and Isaac, Sandy's
real-life tensions are not palliated by fantasy consolations—the
"eggs," the Second Movement of the Jupiter Symphony,
Tracy's face—because he's lost the ability to respond to them.
Stardust Memories seriously questions what the comic does
when he begins to perceive life as tragedy. It's a valid question,
and the further, biographical question of whether successful
comic filmmaker Woody Allen is or is not experiencing a similar dilemma is (not unintentionally) provocative but thematically irrelevant.

Though it's set during one very long Sandy Bates retrospective weekend at the Stardust Hotel, *Stardust Memories* is as
fragmented and chronologically skewed as *Annie Hall.* Childhood, old and present love affairs, black fantasy and painful

reality are arbitrarily interwoven as in an anxious dream. As in *Interiors,* indicative dramatic episodes introduce the main characters: Dorrie (Charlotte Rampling), Sandy's psychotic former lover, who, Tony Roberts is back to inform us, "could be great two days a month, but the other twenty-eight . . ."; Sandy's current French lover Isobel (Marie-Christine Barrault); and concert violinist Daisy (Jessica Harper), who, like Mary in *Manhattan,* identifies herself as "trouble," and may just turn out to be the "perfect woman." We are also swiftly introduced to a gaggle of chauffeurs, to Stardust weekend guests—all demanding favors for themselves or other worthy causes—to film business men and women who would like to append a happy "Jazz Heaven" ending to Sandy's depressing new film. And one of *Stardust Memories'* most darkly funny episodes is a flashback visit to the Brooklyn home of Sandy's sister and brother-in-law. The brother-in-law, feverishly pedaling his stationary bike, is the medical equivalent of artistically luckless Joey. He tells Sandy, "I had two heart attacks before I got the bike." And since? "I also had two heart attacks."

Far more symbolic than the earlier works, *Stardust Memories* invites psychological, mythic, and cinematic comparisons. On one level, it is the tale of a self-despising narcissist who can't see past his own image to derive pleasure elsewhere. It is also the story of a creator who can no longer create—and not, as was the case with Joey, because he hasn't the gift, but because he's lost the will. (Sandy seems to favor the latter interpretation: when accused of narcissism, he ironically retorts that the Greek mythological figure he most closely identifies with is not Narcissus, but Zeus.) Like Frank Capra's *It's a Wonderful Life, Stardust Memories* follows a man who finds life unbearable until confronted with the even less pleasing alternative of death; and as in Preston Sturges's *Sullivan's Travels,* its hero is plagued by the meaninglessness of his comic filmmaking craft.

Visually and thematically, *Stardust Memories* vividly recalls Fellini's *8½:* both Sandy and Fellini's Guido are successful, middle-aged filmmakers who, on the verge of nervous breakdowns, briefly leave their everyday lives, experience cathartic release, and return to reality somewhat reconciled to themselves and their art. And *Stardust Memories* is filled with obliquely perceived American variations on Fellini grotesques. But differences between these films are similarly revealing. While Fellini indulges his grotesques, Allen impartially scrutinizes the Stardust guests, often in ruthless close-up. And *8½*'s warm sensuality finds no answering voice in the almost palpably gelid *Stardust Memories*—in this respect, more like Bergman's than any of Fellini's works.

Analogies between *Stardust Memories* and *Sullivan's Travels* are equally complex. The latter focuses on a Hollywood filmmaker who, convinced that his comedies are frivolous, is determined to create a significant work at last. And a significant film must, he feels, engage the common man's miseries and frustrations, deal realistically with penury, unemployment, and hunger. Possessing no firsthand knowledge of any of the above, Sturges's hero sets out to "take physic, pomp." And while he succeeds in courting miseries beyond his wildest dreams, he also learns that what the common man wants is not a mirror to his troubles, but the release of laughter: so his gifts were not worthless after all. (Interestingly, Allen had never seen *Sullivan's Travels* when he made *Stardust Memories.* When Sturges's son saw Allen's film, he "sent me a print of his father's film," Allen recalls, "and amazingly similar points are covered.")

While *Stardust Memories'* dramatic thrust and message uncannily parallel Sturges's, discrepancies are perhaps more significant here. Accustomed to his Rolls-Royce, sophisticated companionship, and the services of maid, chauffeur, and secretary, Sandy Bates is, in the words of his imagined "superintelligent beings," "not the missionary type." Where Sturges's hero is eager to share the common man's woes, Allen's is as embarrassed by the common man's luckless presence as Mendel is by the hospitalized Meyer. Also like Mendel's, Sandy's good deeds are precipitated by a desire to appear worthy in the eyes of the world and, now more pressingly, to appease his own guilt. One of *Stardust Memories'* most powerful character incongruities is the fact that Sandy is at once sympathetic to various charitable causes—helping the blind, cancer research, Soviet Jewry—and revolted by the people involved. Like Kleinman in "Death," he'd like to give a "cash donation," and like Mendel, he's not seeking truth through reality: he'd like to compensate for reality with a more glorious truth.

So Sandy shares neither Guido's earthy wonder at the carnival of life, nor the Sturges hero's illusions about populist wisdom. For Sandy, carnival and common man are epitomized by the passengers on the train he'd desperately like to get off and by the too short, fat, squint-eyed or long-nosed Stardust guests, burdening and perhaps contaminating him with their failures. And in keeping with its protagonist's perspective, *Stardust Memories'* camera approaches reality warily—often, it seems, through the wrong side of the looking glass, while its thematic observations are among Allen's most challenging to date. Never has Allen watched life from such a compassionless distance; never has he so assiduously dissociated idea from character and narrative detail. Besides opposing the Jewish and Wasp cultures, *Annie Hall*'s split-screen holiday dinner illuminates personal differences between its protagonists. But this human dimension is rarely acknowledged as *Stardust Memories* grapples with conflicting perspectives on a range of new and familiar issues.

Indicative is its approach to the issue of going to jail. Where Sturges's hero is thrust into a crowded cell, where Virgil Starkwell spends most of *Take the Money and Run* trying to avoid the annoying realities of imprisonment, Sandy only briefly experiences the inside of a jail. Yet *Stardust Memories* fully exploits the *idea* of jail to move its two-train allegory onto a social plane. In an early scene, for instance, Isobel tells Sandy (of the Paris 1968 uprisings), "I remember when I was in jail, it was very romantic . . . The workers were not with us; they were fighting for their salaries . . . And we, we were fighting for the spirit of things." So, as with life for the beautiful as opposed to the grotesque people, jail—and, by implication, all social institutions—is experienced differently, now according to one's social class. For the Paris student, toppling society and going to jail were romantic games played out in an interlude between childhood and the acceptance of social privileges. For the workers, these same activities were a practical attempt to glean social privileges. And to stress this class discrepancy, Allen sets his scene in Sandy's Rolls-Royce. Isobel has no sooner finished her speech than a police car beckons them to the side of the road; and while profusely apologizing to famous Sandy, the authorities carry off his chauffeur on mail fraud charges.

Although it feels contrived at the time, this episode pays off later when Sandy himself is confronted for illegal possession of a gun. Fame will now, it seems, finally do this fame-weary man some practical good. "I'm a celebrity," he shamelessly informs the accusing officer. "You can make an exception in my case." But the officer can't, or won't, and as with the two trains disembarking in the same junkyard, chauffeur and employer ultimately find their way to the same jail.

Stardust Memories takes a similarly conflicted, coolly perspicacious attitude toward children. "Kids are nice," Sandy's sister assures him. But her own experiences are not heartening: "The thirteen and fourteen [year-olds] hitchhiked to Texas. I had the police. I don't know their whereabouts . . . The youngest one is selling stolen cameras. I'm worried. I'm worried." And when first glimpsed, Isobel's two pretty blond children are appealingly familial, but later, as they chatter in French during lunch, Sandy finds them annoyingly, claustrophobically familial. Characteristically, neither scene confronts these children as human beings—they are merely avatars.

And so, on very basic levels, are the women in Sandy's life. Dorrie, for instance, is evoked as a collision of schizophrenic fact and Sandy's romantic illusion, a tension that is succinctly described in two visually opposing sequences, almost a juxtaposition of cubism and portraiture. In the first scene, a series of snapshot-like, erratically lit facial images, Dorrie has the fragmented appearance of a Picasso "demoiselle"; whereas a few scenes later, when the camera lingers over her long sunlit body, Dorrie might have been conjured by Ingres or perhaps Whistler. And the warmer, less mysterious Isobel is similarly perceived in abstraction and often in straightforward opposition to Dorrie: generous, blonde, and slightly plump where Dorrie is narcissistic, dark, and slim; likable and willing to make a romantic commitment to Sandy while Dorrie is elusive and sexually arousing "trouble" for him. Most important, as played by the congenial Marie-Christine Barrault (of *Cousin, Cousine*), Isobel looks and acts like the typical comedienne while Dorrie is the stuff of serious, Ingmar Bergmanesque psychological drama.

Significantly, Allen no longer indulges his persona's protests of romantic innocence. Why does "love fade" for him? Why is Sandy, like Isaac before him, a likely candidate for the "August Strindberg Award" for relations with the opposite sex? The answers are only too apparent as Sandy paces in a circle, wearily assuring his latest infatuation, the concert violinist Daisy, that she won't be "trouble" (though he's just learned that she's bisexual) and may be the "perfect woman." It's now clear to Allen, to us, and probably to Sandy as well that he repeats self-destructive love experiences because only "trouble" excites him.

Since the first nightclub act, the persona has been joyously released by fantasy, and since *Love and Death,* he has lived in fear and awe of death. In *Stardust Memories* these two preoccupations, the one apparently compensation for the other, draw slowly, ominously together. Our first indication that something's gone awry with the illusion valve is the darker comedy in sequences like the hostility fantasy. This scene is set up like the bumper car episode in *Annie Hall.* A Stardust guest suggests that all comedians are impelled by feelings of hostility, and Allen cuts to Sandy's fantasy response: a radio announcer direfully intoning, "We interrupt this program to bring you a special bulletin—Sidney Finkelstein's Hostility has escaped"; a giant teddy bear embracing several human victims to death; Sandy's own voice yelping, "My teacher, Miss Reilly . . . My ex-wife and her alimony lawyer! . . ." Yet, though ebulliently funny in concept, this episode does not bring the aggressive, comic release of Alvy attacking the bumper car drivers. For now Allen consciously undermines our pleasure: his images are gray, his setting a snow-engulfed remote forest, his figures sticks—cartoons in a sense, but no longer bearing the mark of whimsy. Humor and flamboyance are similarly undercut in Sandy's fantasy "perfect woman" operation, a sinister variation on the "What Happens During Intercourse?" segment in *Everything You Always Wanted to Know about Sex,* which now seems dramatic worlds away. And just as Sandy travels a physical circle as he courts Daisy, he moves verbally over familiar territory in what might have been a playful dialogue with imagined "super-intelligent beings" from outer space:

> *Sandy:*   Why's there so much suffering?
> *Beings:* This is unanswerable.
> *Sandy:*   Is there a God?
> *Beings:* These are the wrong questions.
> *Sandy:*   Why am I bothering to do anything . . .
>   like make films?
> *Beings:* We like your films—particularly the ear-
>   lier, funnier ones.

Confirming the implications of Allen's *and* Sandy's bleaker humor, two specific fantasy sequences anticipate Sandy's imagined death. Significantly, both involve magic and carry Isaac's cinematic "vanishings" in *Manhattan* a disconcerting step further. In a first scene, Sandy remembers himself as a child magician, "The Great Sandy," pulling flowers from nowhere and vanishing real objects. In the second scene, Sandy imagines his childhood self walking with his mother and then, more precipitously than Isaac, vanishing skyward from the scene.

Thus Allen viscerally prepares for a climax which, as in *Interiors,* will arouse its protagonist from anguished thoughtfulness and indecision. Finally at the end of his tether, Sandy directs his frustrated rage at comedienne Isobel:

> I'm tired of my lawyer and my accountant, and I
> can't help anyone. I can't help the cancer society,
> and I can't help the blind people . . . And I don't
> want to get married now, Isobel. That's the last
> thing I need now is a family and commitment.

As he rejects the trappings and consolations of comedy, Sandy is as exasperating as was Fielding Mellish when he courted these very things many years ago in *Bananas.* Yet, as was similarly true with Fielding, circumstance will show the egregiously flawed Sandy in more sympathetic light. And Sandy's circumstance is now that of the Jimmy Stewart character on the verge of suicide in Frank Capra's *It's a Wonderful Life,* of the narrative voice in Robert Frost's "Birches," who begs that no "fate willfully misunderstand" his fantasy needs and deprive him of reality altogether. For, having finished his speech to Isobel, Sandy is (in his fantasy) murdered by a fan. In reality, he faints and awaits cathartic rebirth.

Although some of its specific narrative details (notably Sandy's apparent reconcilation to life with romantically "untroublesome" Isobel) are improbable, there's superb psychological and dramatic truth to *Stardust Memories'* resolution: to the fact that black magic releases illusion-needing Sandy just as Pearl's kiss of life symbolically revives motherless Joey. As was true with *Interiors, Stardust Memories* favors a compromise. Sandy returns to imperfect life, reconciled not only to reality's and his own limitations, but to the bright half-wrong of the comic interpretation of life wherein lie his artistic gifts. Significantly, Sandy has found an ending to his film, which may just win the approval of the businessmen and find an audience. He describes this new scene to Isobel:

> We're on a train; and there are a million sad people on it. And I have no idea where it's heading. I could be anywhere. It could be the same junkyard . . . But it's not as terrible as I originally thought it was, because, you know, we like each other, and we have some laughs, and there's a lot of closeness . . .

Like Fellini's, Sturges's, and Capra's heroes before him, Sandy Bates finds comfort in the small pleasures of "laughs" and "closeness" and liking someone, and in the big advantage of not being dead. More important, he reasserts his control over and against reality. Thus, *Stardust Memories'* tragic/comic tensions relent, not in the absurdist indominatability of Virgil whittling a soap gun; or the romantic comedy convention of *Bananas'* wedding; or with Alvy Singer still unreasonably hoping for the perfect romance, but with Sandy Bates's rekindled desire to create—and if the medium be comedy, then so be it. While remaining true to his themes, characters, and narrative thrust, Allen here explains his own prodigious "denial of death."

The Floating Lightbulb

In *The Floating Lightbulb,* his first full-length play in a decade, Allen pursues many of the themes of the *Side Effects* stories and *Stardust Memories* within the context of realistic drama. The time is 1945 (when Allen himself was twelve), the setting an apartment in Brooklyn, of which Allen notes: "It is not so much that the apartment is dirty, it is simply that it has been too difficult to keep pace with its rate of decay." And not unlike their apartment, the Pollacks—Enid, Max, and their teenage sons Paul and Steve—are struggling against unfavorable odds. In sharp contrast to Allen's recent protagonists, these are the common men and women of the world, each in his/her own way seeking, as one character suggests, to turn "the everyday into something special." There are no Susan Hollanders or Dick Christies or box-office-minded producers here; though their illusions vary in strength and purity, all these characters are, on one level, illusionists.

The most pedestrian of Allen's dreamers are the boyishly, somewhat raffishly attractive fifty-year-old Max and the Pollacks' younger, quipster son Steve, who shares his father's daredevil predilections. Although Max married the brighter, more ambitious Enid for love, theirs has long been a marriage of mutual recrimination, with his drifting from job to mediocre job, and she ever more acridly, and now alcoholically, insisting she deserves better. A weak rather than an evil man, Max's is the gambler's fantasy of hitting the right number just once and leaving his current waiter's position, his gambling debts, and family behind to start a new life with his "breath of fresh air," young girl friend Betty. Steve's similarly escapist dreams are of leaving school for the excitement of the streets, where he has been known to start fires; while small-time New York talent agent Jerry Wexler, who arrives in Act Two, has long yearned to discover the one performer who will bring him fame and fortune.

Allen's most intense dreamer is Enid, who, for all her specific complaints and get-rich-quick campaigns, longs for the amorphous something extraordinary—for someone to notice that she's still beautiful, for one of her men to succeed glamorously. And stammering sixteen-year-old Paul is Allen's purist dreamer, literally as well as figuratively an illusionist. As did Allen at his age, Paul avoids school to visit magic shops and assiduously practice his tie-splitting, Chinese Water Vase, and, most impressively, his Floating Lightbulb tricks. But autobiographical comparisons finish here. For painfully shy, stuttering Paul hasn't the stamina or drive to envision a real-life application for his art beyond "prrracticing." One model for Paul is a boy Allen remembers from childhood: "I would pass by this particular house, and there was a seventeen-year-old kid who would sit by the window and shuffle cards constantly. He was his mother's cross to bear—there's no question about it."

As it assuredly evokes characters and lays dramatic foundation, the first act of *The Floating Lightbulb,* like *Stardust Memories,* shows pain beneath a patina of brittle humor. Enid returns exhausted from a day of selling hosiery to find Steve headed for trouble in the streets and the more sensitive Paul monkishly secluded with his magic equipment. Max soon appears in a new "jazzy sports shirt," with only four dollars' worth of tips to contribute to the depleted family coffers and unashamedly on his way to meet Betty. "Don't start nagging him," Steve implores Enid. But her son's suggestions go unheeded, and Enid's compulsive, bitterly comic nagging rings throughout the act: why don't her men, and especially Paul with his IQ of 148, "apply" themselves? Why doesn't her wealthier sister Lena appreciate the good sense of supporting Enid's schemes—such as packaging bagels and lox for Jewish families in the South? At act's end, hope presents itself to Enid in the figure of talent agent Jerry Wexler, who agrees to visit and appraise Paul's magic "act" next Tuesday evening. "Opportunity's knocking, and we're in no position to shut it out," Enid warns the unenthusiastic Paul, assuring him that an "act" is only the sum of his best tricks. And to placate Enid, Paul promises to perform.

As in Tennessee Williams's *The Glass Menagerie,* "the gentleman caller's" visit is disastrous, and now on two accounts. With ambition incommensurate to fears, Paul flounders in uncertainty, and his act ends with the shattering of the oriental vase and a liquor bottle as well. Still, as her son retreats to his room, a disappointed but undaunted Enid harks to the call of yet another illusion, this one romantic. For Jerry Wexler, she now learns, finds her "pretty" and then, under the influence of liquor, "beautiful." He understands her angry outbursts: "It only means you're sensitive. Passionate," and furthermore is unmarried because he had as little luck in his search for the right woman as in his more intense quest for a profitable client. And so, as the full moon shines over Canarsie (as it shone over *Our Town*), Enid indulges Jerry's tales of dog acts and vaudevillians, he appreciates her finer qualities, and they share a magic interlude which is broken, as irrevocably as Paul's oriental vase, with Jerry's announcement that he's moving with his asthmatic mother to Phoenix: ". . . Y'know, there comes a time in a man's life when he has to face up to the fact that his plans haven't materialized." Thus, the one character professionally engaged in the arts proves the most pallid dreamer of all.

And after many small hopes have been raised and squelched, *The Floating Lightbulb* ends with real life much the same as it was. Paul is "prrracticing" in his room; Steve begs to be allowed to miss school tomorrow; Max is more determined than ever to leave Brooklyn as soon as possible. The more frustrated for her brief respite from life as it is, Enid moves to strike the exiting Max with Paul's magic cane—and out flutters a bouquet of paper flowers. After contemplating this latest "illusion" for a moment, Enid (in Allen's stage directions) "tosses [the flowers] aside and with a sigh of resignation, rises and begins straightening up, a figure of dignity that has no choice but to go on with life."

Although most acknowledged *The Floating Lightbulb* as deeper and stronger than *Play It Again, Sam,* many critics caviled at its frank indebtedness to Arthur Miller, Tennessee Williams, and Clifford Odets: what happened to the stylistically adventurous "auteur" of *Manhattan* and *Stardust Memories?*

Allen's unapologetic response is that he has no taste for avant-garde or absurdist theater, that his inclinations are toward the realistic plays of Ibsen, Chekhov, and mainstream American dramatists; "if I did another, it would be hopefully deeper," he says, "but just as conventional."

And indeed *The Floating Lightbulb*'s considerable strengths are the conventional ones of powerful themes arising from the interaction of believable characters. Enid, played by Bea Arthur in the original cast, eschews stereotype, growing more fragile and, as was true with Pearl and Tracy, less predictable as the play continues. Her sharp humor is portrayed, like Miles's, as a "defense mechanism," but also as a mark of high-spirited intelligence and sometimes of gentle self-mockery. With his obvious toupée, his whining tales, and flattery that is at once facile and sincere, Jerry (Jack Weston) too is a well-drawn, idiosyncratic variation of the "gentleman caller" model. And Paul (Brian Backer, who won a Tony Award for this performance) is uncompromisingly evoked in opposition to the Allen prototype. Whereas stand-up-comic Woody, Virgil, and Fielding overcame natural timidity, self-disgust, and want of the "classic theatrical suntan" to get up onstage, or into crime or revolution, Paul can't or won't leave his room. Furthermore, though he has the artistic gift, he hasn't the psychological release—and crutch—of humor. Steve, Enid, Max, and Jerry deflect despair not only by deluding, but by comically exorcising themselves: in confirmation of *Stardust Memories'* Hostility fantasy, they vent aggression in bitter wit. But Paul hasn't a funny line in the play.

Beyond its specific virtues, *The Floating Lightbulb* brings into sharp focus many of the ideas Allen's recent work has explored. The importance of luck is again stressed, in the inexorable fact of Paul's shyness, but now in more everyday ways as well. For instance, what if Enid and Jerry had met before he decided to move to Phoenix? Both of their lives might have been different. And *The Floating Lightbulb* observes a discrepancy between art and performance suggested by Joey's reconcilation to diary-writing. For unlike Joey, Paul has the ability, the gift, to create illusion; and yet his talents are obscured by stuttering shyness and shaking hands when he's forced to conjure for others. Indicative is a discussion in which Enid tries to convince Paul that performing is easy:

> Enid.   Do you think any of those clowns earning
>   a fortune pulling rabits out of hats is any

> better than you? Certainly not! They're all
> just ordinary men like you see every day,
> except they've practiced a little and they
> have the brains to dress up in a tuxedo and
> a turban and instead of Joe Blow, call them-
> selves The Great Mysterioso.

Paul. I—wouldn't kn-know how to begin.

Enid. Excuses, excuses! And what is it? It's right
> here, in your own living room, in front of
> your family and one other nice, friendly
> man.

Paul. That's the part th-that m-makes me ner-
> vous. The friendly m-man.

And Paul is right in the end. He can create splendor alone in
his room, but only chaos before "the friendly man."

Of all Allen's recent work, *The Floating Lightbulb* most
diaphanously contemplates the reality/fantasy conflict. As in
Stardust Memories, magic is subtly equated with death—now
when the world-weary Enid proclaims, "I want to vanish." And
even more than in the film, discrepancies between real life and
illusion, between "people cashing in" and "heaven and angels
and saints" are trenchantly questioned. For instance, Enid's
idea of turning Paul's passion into a vocation *sounds* realistic.
But in light of psychological handicaps, this idea is a good deal
less practical than transporting Jewish brunches to the South.
In fact it's harmful, and Enid acknowledges as much when
she confesses to Jerry: "I push [Paul] too hard . . . I know
it . . ." And, on the other hand, while Max *seems* to be shirking
realistic duties to his family in favor of a dream of beginning
again, mightn't this apparent desertion, like Joey's and Sandy
Bates's fresh starts, prove the best, most practical answer to a
loveless marriage?

In pronounced contrast to Allen's earlier work, *Interiors,
Stardust Memories,* and *The Floating Lightbulb* favor the
dreamer's compromise with reality: first, because there are
compensations of "laughs" and "closeness," because it's only
"awful," like the food in the Catskills, and not really terrible,
like "vanishing" and Boris's "worse than the food at Kresge's"
fate; and finally because he has no choice. The darker vision of

a now-middle-aged artist seems more attuned to life's limitations. And yet, as has been true with Allen from the start, answers are not that simple. At the end of _Interiors_ and _Stardust Memories,_ the protagonist is defiantly creating. In a final, quizzical shot of Isaac, in _Manhattan,_ he is perversely, unreasonably hopeful. And just before she goes back to the business of surviving, Enid looks hard and long at her bouquet of paper flowers.

At one point in _The Floating Lightbulb,_ Enid tells Paul that magic is "wonderful," but "there's a practical side to life that must be dealt with." And as her words drum home this play's message, they evoke memories of all Allen's earlier work as well. We remember stand-up-comic Woody, in "The Great Renaldo," torn between his "magic" role as a fire engine and his reality as a little man caught out on a Sunday night in his red pajamas. We can almost _see_ Virgil Starkwell's soap escape gun "dealing with" the real rain and fizzling into bubbles. And what of Fielding Mellish defying his "real" loser self in _Bananas,_ posing as El Presidente, and winning the girl? They may even live happily ever after: "Again, they may not."

Enid's words also bring to mind what in retrospect seems the turning point in Allen's art: the death of Boris in _Love and Death_—the painlessness of comedy having "dealt with" and succumbed to real life inevitabilities. Or was the turning point in fact with _Annie Hall,_ where Allen unequivocally states that "love fades," though we need to believe otherwise?

Certainly, Allen's confrontations have grown increasingly serious since _Love and Death_ and _Annie Hall:_ but the change is only a sea change. Though his art has darkened and deepened, Allen has not denied the urges of early stand-up-comic Woody, who outlived the doorman's attack only to get hypnotized by "The Ed Sullivan Show." And if Allen's protagonists are no longer, as in "The Great Renaldo," running down Fifth Avenue in their red pajamas, they are still looking for the fire.

Appendix I

Filmography

What's New, Pussycat? (1965)

Director: Clive Donner. Producer: Charles K. Feldman. Screenplay: Woody Allen. Photography: Jean Badal (Technicolor, Scope). Music: Burt Bacharach. Editor: Fergus McDonell. Sound: William-Robert Sivel. Art Director: Jacques Saulnier. Assistant Director: Enrico Isacco. Special Effects: Bob MacDonald. A Famous Artists Production. 120 minutes.

Peter Sellers (Fritz Fassbender). Peter O'Toole (Michael James). Romy Schneider (Carol Werner). Capucine (Renée Lefebvre). Paula Prentiss (Liz Bien). Woody Allen (Victor Shakapopolis). Ursula Andress (Rita). Edra Gale (Anna Fassbender). Catherine Schaake (Jacqueline). Jess Hahn (Perry Werner). Eleanor Hirt (Sylvia Werner). Nicole Karen (Tempest O'Brien). Jean Paredes (Marcel). Michel Subor (Philippe). Jacqueline Fogt (Charlotte). Robert Rollis (Car Renter). Daniel Emilfork (Gas Station Attendant). Louis Falavigna (Jean, his friend). Jacques Balutin (Etienne). Annette Poivre (Emma). Sabine Sun (Nurse). Jean Yves Autrey, Pascal Wolf, Nadine Papin (Fassbender children). Tanya Lopert (Miss Lewis). Colin Drake (Durell), Norbert Terry (Kelly). F. Medard (Nash). Gordon Felio (Fat Man). Louise Lasser (The Nutcracker). Richard Saint-Bris (Mayor). Françoise Hardy (Mayor's secretary). Douking (Renée's concierge).

What's Up, Tiger Lily? (1966)

Original version: *Kagi No Kagi (Key of Keys),* (Japan, 1964). Director: Senkichi Taniguchi. Script: Hideo Ando. Photography: Kazuo Yamada (Eastmancolor, Scope). Produced by Tomoyuki Tanaka for Toho. 94 minutes.

Re-release Director: Woody Allen. Production Conception: Ben Shapiro. Editor: Richard Krown. Script and Dubbing: Woody Allen, Frank Buxton, Len Maxwell, Louise Lasser, Mickey Rose, Julie Bennett, Bryna Wilson. Music: The Lovin' Spoonful. 79 minutes.

Tatsuya Mihashi (Phil Moskowitz). Mie Hana (Terry Yaki). Akiko Wakayabayashi (Suki Yaki). Tadao Nakamaru (Shepherd Wong). Susumu Kurobe (Wing Fat).

Casino Royale (1967)

Directors: John Huston, Kenneth Hughes, Val Guest, Robert Parrish, Joseph McGrath. Producers: Charles K. Feldman and Jerry Bresler. Screenplay: Wolf Mankowitz, John Law, Michael Sayers, suggested by the novel by Ian Fleming. Photography: Jack Hildyard (Panavision, Technicolor). Editor: Bill Lenny. Production Designer: Michael Ayringer. Special Effects: Cliff Richardson, Roy Whybrow. Music: Burt Bacharach. Titles, Montage: Richard Williams. A Famous Artists Production, released by Columbia Pictures. 131 minutes.

Peter Sellers (Evelyn Tremble). Ursula Andress (Vesper Lynd). David Nivin (Sir James Bond). Orson Welles (Le Chiffre). Joanna Pettet (Mata Bond). Deborah Kerr (Widow McTarry). Daliah Lavi (The Detainer). Woody Allen (Jimmy Bond). William Holden (Ransome). Charles Boyer (Le Grand). John Huston (M). Kurt Kaznar (Smernov). George Raft (Himself). Jean-Paul Belmondo (French Legionnaire). Terence Cooper (Cooper). Barbara Bouchet (Moneypenny). Angela Scoular (Buttercup). Gabriella Licudi (Eliza). Tracey Crisp (Heather). Jacky Bisset (Miss Goodthings). Anna Quayle (Frau Hoffner). Derek Nimmo (Hadley). Ronnie Corbett (Polo). Colin Gordon (Casino Director). Bernard Cribbens (Taxi Driver). Tracy Reed (Fang Leader). Duncan Macrae (Inspector Mathis). Graham Stark (Cashier). Richard Wattis (British Army Officer). Percy Herbert (First Piper).

Don't Drink the Water (1969)

Director: Howard Morris. Producer: Charles Joffe. Screenplay: R. S. Allen and Harvey Bullock, based upon the stageplay by Woody Allen. Photography: Harvey Genkins (Movielab, color). Music: Pat Williams. Art Director: Robert Gundlach. Editor: Ralph Rosenblum. Assistant Director: Louis Stroller. 98 minutes.

Jackie Gleason (Walter Hollander). Estelle Parsons (Marion Hollander). Ted Bessell (Axel Magee). Joan Delaney (Susan Hollander). Richard Libertini (Drobney). Michael Costantine (Krojack). Avery Schreiber (Sultan). Also: Howard St. John, Danny Mehan, Pierre Olaf, Phil Leeds, Mark Gordon, Dwayne Early, Joan Murphy, Martin Danzig, Rene Constantineau, Howard Morris.

Take the Money and Run (1969)

Director: Woody Allen. Script: Woody Allen and Mickey Rose. Photography: Lester Shorr (Technicolor). Editing: Paul Jordan, Ron Kalish. Music: Marvin Hamlisch. Art Director: Fred Harpman. Special Effects: A. D. Flowers. Assistant Directors: Louis Stroller, Walter Hill. Produced by Charles H. Joffe for Palomar Pictures. 85 minutes.

Woody Allen (Virgil Starkwell). Janet Margolin (Louise). Marcel Hillaire (Fritz). Jacqueline Hyde (Miss Blair). Lonnie Chapman (Jake). Jan Merlin (Al). James Anderson (Chain gang warden). Howard Storm (Red). Mark Gordon (Vince). Micil Murphy (Frank). Minnow Moskowitz (Joe Agneta). Nate Jacobson (Judge). Grace Bauer (Farm-house lady). Ethel Sokolow (Mother Starkwell). Henry Leff (Father Starkwell). Don Frazier (Psychiatrist). Mike O'Dowd (Michael Sullivan). Jackson Beck (Narrator). Louise Lasser (Kay Lewis).

Bananas (1971)

Director: Woody Allen. Script: Woody Allen and Mickey Rose. Photography: Andrew M. Costikyan (Deluxe Color). Production Designer: Ed Wittstein. Music: Marvin Hamlisch. Editor: Ron Kalish. Associate Producer: Ralph Rosenblum. Assistant Director: Fred T. Gallo. Special Effects: Don B. Courtney. Produced by Jack Grossberg for Rollins and Joffe Productions. 81 minutes.

Woody Allen (Fielding Mellish). Louise Lasser (Nancy). Carlos Montalban (General Vargas). Natividad Abascal (Yolanda). Jacobo Morales (Esposito). Miguel Suarez (Luis). David Ortiz (Sanchez). Rene Enriquez (Diaz). Jack Axelrod (Arroyo). Howard Cosell (Himself). Roger Grimsby (Himself). Don Dunphy (Himself). Charlotte Rae (Mrs. Mellish). Stanley Ackerman (Dr. Mellish). Dan Frazer (Priest). Martha Greenhouse (Dr. Feigen). Axel Anderson (man tortured). Tigre Perez (Perez). Baron de Beer (British ambassador). Arthur Hughes (Judge). John Braden (Prosecutor). Ted Chapman (Policeman). Dorthi Fox (J. Edgar Hoover). Dagne Crane (Sharon). Ed Barth (Paul). Nicholas Saunders (Douglas). Conrad Bain (Semple). Eulogio Peraza (Interpreter). Norman Evans (Senator). Robert O'Connel and Robert Dudley (FBI). Marilyn Hengst (Norma). Ed Crowley and Beeson Carroll (FBI Security). Allen Garfield (Man on cross). Princess Fatosh (Snakebite lady). Dick Callinan (Ad man). Hy Anzel (Patient).

Play It Again, Sam (1972)

Director: Herbert Ross. Production Supervisor: Roger M. Rothstein. Screenplay: Woody Allen, based on his stageplay. Photography: Owen Roizman (Technicolor). Music: Billy Goldenberg. Editor: Marion Rothman. Assistant Director: William Gerrity. An Arthur P. Jacobs Production for Paramount Pictures. 84 minutes.

Woody Allen (Allan Felix). Diane Keaton (Linda). Tony Roberts (Dick). Jerry Lacy (Bogart). Susan Anspach (Nancy). Jennifer Salt (Sharon). Joy Bang (Julie). Viva (Jennifer). Suzanne Zenor (Discotheque girl). Diana Davila (Museum girl). Mari Fletcher (Fantasy Sharon). Michael Green and Ted Markland (Hoods).

*Everything You Always Wanted To Know About Sex**
*(*but were afraid to ask)* (1972)

Director: Woody Allen. Script: Woody Allen, from the book by David Reuben. Photography: David M. Walsh (DeLuxe Color). Assistant Directors: Fred T. Gallo, Terry M. Carr. Editor: Eric Albertson. Music: Mundell Lowe. Production Design: Dale Hennesy. Produced by Charles H. Joffe for United Artists. 87 minutes.

Woody Allen (Fool, Fabrizio, Victor, Sperm). John Carradine (Dr. Bernardo). Lou Jacobi (Sam). Louise Lasser (Gina). Anthony Quayle (King). Tony Randall (Operator). Lynne Redgrave (Queen). Burt Reynolds (Switchboard). Gene Wilder (Dr. Ross). Jack Barry (Himself). Erin Fleming (The Girl). Elaine Giftos (Mrs. Ross). Toni Holt (Herself). Robert Q. Lewis (Himself). Heather Macrae (Helen). Pamela Mason (Herself). Sidney Miller (George). Regis Philbin (Himself). Titos Vandis (Milos). Stanley Adams (Stomach operator). Oscar Beregi (Brain control). Alan Caillou (Fool's father). Dort Clark (Sheriff). Geoffrey Holder (Sorcerer). Jay Robinson (Priest). Ref Sanchez (Igor). Don Chuy and Tom Mack (football players). Baruch Lumet (Rabbi Baumel). Robert Walden (Sperm). H. E. West (Bernard Jaffe).

Sleeper (1973)

Director: Woody Allen. Script: Woody Allen, Marshall Brickman. Photography: David M. Walsh (DeLuxe Color). Editor: Ralph Rosenblum. Production Designer: Dale Hennesy. Assistant Directors: Fred T. Gallo, Henry J. Lange, Jr. Special Effects: A. D. Flowers. Music by Woody Allen with the Preservation Hall Jazz Band and the New Orleans Funeral Ragtime Orchestra. Dr. Melik's house designed by Charles Deaton, architect. Produced by Jack Grossberg for Jack Rollins and Charles Joffe Productions. 88 minutes.

Woody Allen (Miles Monroe). Diane Keaton (Luna Schlosser). John Beck (Erno Windt). Mary Gregory (Dr. Melik). Don Keefer (Dr. Tryon). John McLiam (Dr. Agon). Bartlett Robinson (Dr. Orva). Chris Forbes (Rainer Krebs). Marya Small (Dr. Nero). Peter Hobbs (Dr. Dean). Susan Miller (Ellen Pogrebin). Lou Picetti (Master of Ceremonies). Jessica Rains (Woman in the mirror). Brian Avery (Herald Cohen). Spencer Milligan (Jeb Hrmthmg) [sic]. Stanley Ross (Sears Swiggles).

Love and Death (1975)

Director: Woody Allen. Photography: Ghislain Cloquet (DeLuxe Color). Script: Woody Allen. Editing: Ralph Rosenblum, Ron Kalish. Assistant Directors: Paul Feyder, Bernard Cohn. Special Effects: Kit West. Music: S. Prokofiev. Art Director: Willy Holt. Costume Designer: Gladys De Segonzac.

Produced by Charles H. Joffe for Jack Rollins and Charles H. Joffe Productions. 85 minutes.

Woody Allen (Boris). Diane Keaton (Sonia). Georges Adet (Old Nehamken). Frank Adu (Drill sergeant). Edmond Ardisson (Priest). Feodor Atkine (Mikhail). Albert Augier (Waiter). Yves Barsaco (Rimsky). Lloyd Battista (Don Francisco). Jack Berard (General Lecoq). Eva Bertrand (Woman in hygiene lesson). George Birt (Doctor). Yves Brainville (Andre). Gerard Buhr (Servant). Brian Coburn (Dmitri). Henri Coutet (Minskov). Patricia Crown (Cheerleader). Henry Czarniak (Ivan). Despo Diamantidou (Mother). Sandor Eles (Soldier). Luce Fabiole (Grandmother). Florian (Uncle Nikolai). Jacqueline Fogt (Ludmilla). Sol L. Frieder (Voskovec). Olga Georges-Picot (Countess Alexandrovna). Harold Gould (Count Anton). Harry Hankin (Uncle Sasha). Jessica Harper (Natasha). Tony Jan (Vladimir Maximovitch). Tutte Lemkow (Pierre). Jack Lenoir (Krapotkin). Leib Lensky (Father Andre). Ann Lonnberg (Olga). Roger Lumont (Baker). Alfred Lutter III (Young Boris). Ed Marcus (Raskov). Jacques Maury (Second). Narcissa McKinley (Cheerleader). Aubrey Morris (Soldier). Denise Peron (Spanish Countess). Beth Porter (Anna). Alan Rossett (Guard). Shimen Ruskin (Borslov). Persival Russel (Berdykov). Chris Sanders (Joseph). Zvee Scooler (Father). C. A. R. Smith (Father Nikolai). Fred Smith (Soldier). Bernard Taylor (Soldier). Clement-Thierry (Jacques). Alan Tilvern (Sergeant). James Tolkan (Napoleon). Helene Vallier (Madame Wolfe). Howard Vernon (General Leveque). Glenn Williams (Soldier). Jacob Witkin (Sushkin).

The Front (1976)

Produced and Directed by Martin Ritt. Script: Walter Bernstein, Music: Dave Grusin. Photography: Michael Chapman (Panavision color). Art Director: Charles Bailey. Editor: Sidney Levin. Assistant Directors: Peter Scoppa, Ralph Singleton. A Martin Ritt-Jack Rollins-Charles H. Joffe Production, distributed by Columbia Pictures. 94 minutes.

Woody Allen (Howard Prince). Zero Mostel (Hecky Brown). Herschel Bernardi (Phil Sussman). Michael Murphy (Alfred Miller). Andrea Marcovicci (Florence Barrett). Remak Ramsay (Hennessey). Marvin Lichterman (Myer Prince). Lloyd Gough (Delaney). David Margulies (Phelps). Joshua Shelley (Sam). Norman Rose (Howard's Attorney). Charles Kimbrough (Committee Counselor). M. Josef Sommer (Committee Chairman). Danny Aiello (Danny La Gattuta). Georgann Johnson (TV interviewer). Scott McKay (Hampton). David Clarke (Hubert Jackson). J. W. Klein (Bank teller). John Bentley (Bartender). Julie Garfield (Margo). Murray Moston (Boss). McIntyre Dixon (Harry Stone). Rudolph Wilrich (Tailman). Burt Britton (Bookseller). Albert M. Ottenheimer (School principal). William Bogert (Parks). Joey Faye (Waiter). Marilyn Sokol (Sandy). John J. Slater (TV director). Renee Paris (Girl in hotel lobby). Joan Porter (Stage-hand). Andrew and Jacob Bernstein (Alfred's children). Matthew Tobin (Man at party). Marilyn Persky (His date). Sam McMurray (Young man at party). Joe Jamrog and Michael Miller (FBI men). Jack Davidson and Donald Symington (Congressmen). Patrick McNamara (Federal Marshal).

Woody Allen: An American Comedy (1977)

Produced and Directed by Harold Mantell, for Films for the Humanities, Inc. (P.O. Box 2053, Princeton, N.J., 08540). Narrated by Woody Allen. 30 minutes.

Annie Hall (1977)

Director: Woody Allen. Script: Woody Allen and Marshall Brickman. Photography: Gordon Willis (Panavision DeLuxe). Editor: Ralph Rosenblum. Art Director: Mel Bourne. Animated Sequences: Chris Ishii. Assistant Directors: Fred T. Gallo, Fred Blankfein. Costume Designer: Ruth Morley. Produced by Charles H. Joffe for Jack Rollins and Charles H. Joffe Productions. Distributed by United Artists. 93 minutes.

Woody Allen (Alvy Singer). Diane Keaton (Annie Hall). Tony Roberts (Rob). Carol Kane (Allison). Paul Simon (Tony Lacy). Shelley Duvall (Pam). Janet Margolin (Robin). Colleen Dewhurst (Mom Hall). Christopher Walken (Duane). Donald Symington (Dad Hall). Helen Ludlam (Granny Hall). Mordecai Lawner (Alvy's father). Joan Newman (Alvy's mother). Jonathan Munk (Alvy, aged 9). Ruth Volner (Alvy's aunt). Martin Rosenblatt (Alvy's uncle). Hy Ansel (Joey Nichols). Rashel Novikoff (Aunt Tessie). Russell Horton (Man in theater line). Marshall McLuhan (Himself). Christine Jones (Dorrie). Mary Boylan (Miss Reed). Wendy Girard (Janet). John Doumanian (Coke fiend). Bob Maroff and Rick Petrucelli (Men outside theater). Lee Callahan (Ticket-seller at theater). Chris Gampel (Doctor). Dick Cavett (Himself). Mark Leonard (Navy Officer). Dan Ruskin (Comedian at rally). John Glover (Actor boyfriend). Bernie Styles (Comic's agent). Johnny Haymer (Comic). Ved Bandhu (Maharishi). John Dennis Johnston (Los Angeles Policeman). Lauri Bird (Tony Lacy's girlfriend). Jim McKrell, Jeff Goldblum, William Callaway, Roger Newman, Alan Landers, Jean Sarah Frost (Lacy's party guests). Vince O'Brien (Hotel Doctor). Humphrey Davis (Alvy's psychiatrist). Veronica Radburn (Annie's psychiatrist). Robin Mary Paris (Actress in rehearsal). Charles Levin (Actor in rehearsal). Wayne Carson (Rehearsal stage manager). Michael Karm (Rehearsal director). Petronia Johnson, Shaun Casey (Tony's dates at nightclub). Ricardo Bertoni, Michael Aronin (Waiters at nightclub). Lou Picetti, Loretta Tupper, James Burge, Shelly Hack, Albert Ottenheimer, Paula Trueman (Street strangers). Beverly D'Angelo, Tracey Walter (Stars in Rob's TV show). David Wier, Keith Dentice, Susan Mellinger, Hamit Perezic, James Balter, Eric Gould, Amy Levitan (Alvy's classmates). Gary Allen, Frank Vohs, Sybil Bowan, Margaretta Warwick (Teachers). Lucy Lee Flippen (Health Food waitress). Gary

Muledeer (Man at restaurant). Sigourney Weaver (Alvy's date outside theater). Walter Bernstein (Annie's date outside theater). Artie Butler (Annie's
accompanist).

Interiors (1978)

Written and Directed by Woody Allen. Photography: Gordon Willis. Editor:
Ralph Rosenblum. Production Designer: Mel Bourne. Assistant Director:
Martin Berman. Costume Designer: Joel Schumacher. Produced by Charles
H. Joffe for Jack Rollins-Charles H. Joffe Productions. Distributed by United
Artists. 93 minutes.
    Kristen Griffith (Flynn). Marybeth Hurt (Joey). Richard Jordan (Freder-
ick). Diane Keaton (Renata). E. G. Marshall (Arthur). Geraldine Page (Eve).
Maureen Stapleton (Pearl). Sam Waterston (Mike).

Manhattan (1979)

Director: Woody Allen. Script: Woody Allen and Marshall Brickman. Pho-
tography: Gordon Willis (black and white). Editor: Susan E. Morse. Produc-
tion Designer: Mel Bourne. Costumes: Albert Wolsky. Music by George
Gershwin, adapted and arranged by Tom Pierson; performed by the New
York Philharmonic, conducted by Zubin Mehta, and the Buffalo Philhar-
monic, conducted by Michael Tilson Thomas. Assistant Directors: Fredric B.
Blankfein, Joan Spiegel Feinstein. Executive Producer: Robert Greenhut.
Produced by Charles H. Joffe for Rollins-Joffe Productions. Distributed by
United Artists. 96 minutes.
    Woody Allen (Isaac Davis). Diane Keaton (Mary Wilke). Michael Murphy
(Yale). Mariel Hemingway (Tracy). Meryl Streep (Jill). Anne Byrne (Emily).
Karen Ludwig (Connie). Michael O'Donoghue (Dennis). Victor Truro, Tisa
Farrow, Helen Hanft (party guests). Bella Abzug (guest of honor). Gary
Weis, Kenny Vance (TV producers)). Charles Levin, Karen Allen, David
Rasche (TV actors). Damion Sheller (Willie). Wallace Shawn (Jeremiah).
Mark Linn Baker, Frances Conroy (Shakespearean actors). Bill Anthony,
John Doumanian (Porsche owners). Ray Serra (pizzeria waiter). "Waffles"
trained by Dawn Animal Agency.

Stardust Memories (1980)

Written and Directed by Woody Allen. Photography: Gordon Willis. Editor:
Susan E. Morse. Production Designer: Mel Bourne. Costumes: Santo Lo-
quasto. Assistant Director: Fredric B. Blankfein. Executive Producers: Jack
Rollins and Charles H. Joffe. Produced by Robert Greenhut for Rollins-Joffe
Productions. Distributed by United Artists. 89 minutes.
    Woody Allen (Sandy Bates). Charlotte Rampling (Dorrie). Jessica Harper
(Daisy). Marie-Christine Barrault (Isobel). Tony Roberts (Tony). Daniel

Stern (actor). Amy Wright (Shelley). Helen Hanft (Vivian Orkin). John Roth-
man (Jack Abel). Anne DeSalvo (Sandy's sister). Joan Neuman (Sandy's
mother). Ken Chapin (Sandy's father). Leonardo Cimino (Sandy's analyst).
Eli Mintz (Old man). Bob Maroff (Jerry Abraham). Gabrielle Strasun (Char-
lotte Ames). David Lipman (George, Sandy's chauffeur). Robert Munk (Boy
Sandy). Jaqui Safra (Sam). Sharon Stone (Pretty girl on train). Andy Albeck,
Robert Friedman, Douglas Ireland, Jack Rollins (Studio executives). Howard
Kissel (Sandy's manager). Max Leavitt (Sandy's doctor). Renee Lippin
(Sandy's press agent). Sol Lomita (Sandy's accountant). Irving Metzman
(Sandy's lawyer). Dorothy Leon (Sandy's cook). Roy Brocksmith (Dick
Lobel). Simon Newey (Mr. Payson). Victoria Zussin (Mrs. Payson). Frances
Pole (Libby). Bill Anthony, Filomena Spagnuolo, Ruth Rugoff, Martha
Whitehead (Fans—hotel arrival). Judith Roberts (Singer—"Three Little
Words"). Barry Weiss (Dancer—"Three Little Words"). Robin Ruinsky,
Adrian Richards, Dominick Petrolino, Sharon Brous, Michael Zannella,
Doris Dugan Slater, Michael Goldstein, Niel Napolitan (Questions askers—
screening). Stanley Ackerman (Reporter—Screening). Noel Behn (Doug
Orkin). Candy Loving (Tony's girlfriend). Denice Danon, Sally Demay, Tom
Dennis, Edward Kotkin, Laura Delano, Lisa Friedman, Brent Spiner, Garde-
nia Cole, Maurice Shrog, Larry Roberts Carr, Brian Zoldessy, Melissa Slade,
Paula Raflo, Jordan Derwin, Tony Azito, Marc Murray, Helen Hale, Carl
Dorn, Victoria Page, Bert Michaels, Deborah Johnson (Fans in lobby). Benja-
min Rayson (Dr. Paul Pearlstein), Mary Mims (Claire Schaeffer). Charles
Lowe (Vaudeville singer). Marie Lane (Cabaret singer—"Brazil"). Gustave
Tassell (Cabaret patrons). Marina Schiano, Dimitri Vassilopoulos, Judith
Crist, Carmin Mastrin (Cabaret patrons). Sylvia Davis (Hostility victim).
Joseph Summo (Hostility). Victor Truro (Hostility psychoanalyst). Irwin
Keyes, Bonnie Hellman, Patrick Daly, Joe Pagano, Wayne Maxwell, Ann
Freeman, Bob Miranti (Fans outside hotel). Cindy Gibb, Manuella Machado
(Young girl fans). Judith Cohen, Madeline Moroff, Maureen P. Levins
(Friends of Sandy's sister). E. Brian Dean (Police sergeant arresting George).
Marvin Peisner (Ed Rich). Robert Tennenhouse, Leslie Smith, Samuel
Chodorov (Autograph seekers on boardwalk). Philip Lenkowsky (Autograph
seeker/assassin). Vanina Holasek (Isobel's daughter). Michel Touchard (Iso-
bel's son). Kenny Vance, Iryn Steinfink (New studio executives). Frank Mo-
dell (Rewrite man). Anne Korzen (Woman in ice cream parlor). Eric Van
Valkenburg (Man in ice cream parlor). Susan Ginsburg (Usherette). Ostaro
(Astrologer). Wade Barnes, Gabriel Barre, Charles Riggs III, Geoffrey Riggs,
Martha Sherrill, Ann Risley, Jade Bari, Marc Geller, Daniel Friedman,
James Otis, Judy Goldner, Rebecca Wright, Perry Gewertz, Larry Fishman,
Liz Albrecht, Sloane Bosniak, James Harter, Henry House, Largo Woodruff,
Jerry Tov Greenberg, Mohammid Nabi Kiani (UFO followers). Alice Spivak
(Nurse at hospital). Armin Shimerman, Edith Grossman, Jacqueline French
(Eulogy audience). John Doumanian (Armenian fan), Jack Hollander (Cop
arresting Sandy).

Appendix 2

Books and Plays

Books

Getting Even, Random House, 1971.
Without Feathers, Random House, 1975.
Side Effects, Random House, 1980.

Plays

Don't Drink the Water, a comedy in two acts by Woody Allen. Directed by Stanley Prager, produced by David Merrick in association with Jack Rollins and Charles Joffe, at the Morosco Theatre, New York City, November 17, 1966.

Original Cast (In Order of Appearance)

Father Drobney	Dick Libertine
Ambassador Magee	House Jameson
Kilroy	Gerry Matthews
Axel Magee	Anthony Roberts
Marion Hollander	Kay Medford
Walter Hollander	Lou Jacobi
Susan Hollander	Anita Gillette
Krojack	James Kukas
Burns	Curtis Wheeler
Chef	Gene Varrone
Sultan of Bashir	Oliver Clark
Sultan's First Wife	Donna Mills
Kasnar	John Hallow
Countess Bordoni	Sharon Talbot
Novotny	Luke Andreas
Walter	Johathan Bolt

Play It Again, Sam, a comedy in three acts by Woody Allen. Presented by David Merrick, in association with Jack Rollins and Charles Joffe, at the Broadhurst Theatre, New York City, February 12, 1969.

Original Cast (In Order of Appearance)

Allan Felix	Woody Allen
Nancy	Sheila Sullivan
Bogey	Jerry Lacey
Dick Christie	Anthony Roberts
Linda Christie	Diane Keaton
Sharon	Barbara Brownell
Sharon Lake	Diana Walker
Gina	Jean Fowler
Vanessa	Cynthia Dalbey
Go-Go Girl	Lee Anne Fahey
Intellectual Girl	Barbara Press
Barbara	Barbara Brownell

The Floating Lightbulb, a drama in two acts by Woody Allen. Directed by Ulu Grosbard, produced by Richmond Crinkley for the Lincoln Center Theater Company, at the Vivian Beaumont Theatre, New York City, April 27, 1981.

Original Cast (In Order of Appearance)

Paul Pollack	Brian Backer
Steve Pollack	Eric Gurry
Enid Pollack	Beatrice Arthur
Max Pollack	Danny Aiello
Betty	Ellen March
Jerry Wexler	Jack Weston

Index